Praise for *Here I Am a Writer*

"For more than twenty years, Kit McIlroy and ArtsReach
have been within the Indigenous voice of the Tohono O'odham
and Yaqui languages in the desert region of Tucson in Southern
Arizona. And in the on-going, dynamic tradition of the oral
languages of Indigenous American peoples, that actually means
"being forever within the voice" since languages of Indigenous
cultural oral traditions are always in creative flux. *Here I
Am a Writer* is a reflection, expression, and exercise of that
dynamic tradition. Put into written form by Tohono O'odham
and Yaqui tribal youth, this literary anthology is composed of
poems, stories, anecdotes, and narrative tellings. Originated
as notebook jottings, journal entries, classroom assignments,
or as hearsay, gossip, and notes passed back and forth, they, by
virtue of ArtsReach guidance, resulted in finely honed pieces
of literature representative of the present-day cultural and
language communities of Tohono O'odham and Yaqui people as
verbalized by their youth. And then over the years published in
the ArtsReach annual collections of *Dancing with the Wind*. And
now resulting in *Here I Am a Writer*, a moving, powerful voice
that evolves from the dynamic traditions of on-going Indigenous
languages that are always changing. Highly recommended!"
—Simon J. Ortiz, author of *Men on the Moon,
Beyond the Reach of Time and Change, Out There Somewhere*

"Kit McIlroy's book beautifully showcases the poetry and
the lives of Native Americans who, as children, participated in
ArtReach, a creative writing project McIlroy founded in 1986.
McIlroy finds his participants, now adults, and shows them—
shows us—their stories and poems, and asks them to reflect
on what their writing meant to them as children and what it
means to them now. Some have careers or steady jobs, one is in
and out of prison, others have died, and some have children of
their own. Wherever McIlroy finds them, they are surprised by

their childhood innocence, and many don't recognize their own writing.

"What we do not get, thankfully, is a quantitative analysis of the effect of writing; rather we see what McIlroy sets out to explore: the "effect it has on the soul." McIlroy weaves the complex stories of their lives with the poems and stories they wrote as children. This is indeed a book that allows us to see the effect of writing on children, not through test scores, but through their writing—through their imaginations."

—Terry Ann Thaxton, Director
The Literary Arts Partnership, University of Central Florida

"*Here I Am a Writer* tells several stories at once, in multiple voices, and what emerges is a moving portrait of people's lives. Christopher McIlroy's long history of teaching creative writing to Native American children is the backdrop, but the narrative that emerges is carried by the words of these children and the adults they become. I know of no other book quite like this. It's a wonder."

—Robert Boswell, author of story collections and novels, including *The Heyday of the Insensitive Bastards*, *Mystery Ride*, *Century's Son*, and nonfiction such as *The Half-Known World*

"This is such a needed book for teachers who work with native kids, but for teachers everywhere. It's like a multigenre reflection piece…It's the perfect example of how writing becomes the window to see outside of ourselves and the mirror by which we look inward at ourselves, and that forever changes us in some ways… The final section where McIlroy shares the techniques that can be used by others is wonderful."

—Robert Wortman, former teacher, principal, and director of Title One, Literacy, and School Improvement for Tucson Unified School District

*Here I Am a Writer*

# Here I Am a Writer

Christopher McIlroy

*Hedda —*
*Memorable stories and poems*
*to add to your memories of*
*Arizona*

*Kit McIlroy*

**Kitsune Books**
*Quality books for eclectic readers*

*Here I Am a Writer*

Kitsune Books
P.O. Box 1154
Crawfordville, FL 32326-1154
www.kitsunebooks.com
contact@kitsunebooks.com

Printed in USA.  First printing 2011

ISBN: 978-0-9827409-1-0
Library of Congress Control Number:  2010935537

Cover artists:
(Yaqui) Marcelino Flores, "New Morning"
(Tohono O'odham) Jeffery Antone, Sr., "Man in the Maze"

Internal student spot art: Robert Arredondo, Angela Francisco, Dionne Lopez, Lorianne Narcho, Bernadette Pablo

◎ ◎ ◎ ◎ ◎ ◎

*For Kelsey*

# Acknowledgements

I owe the deepest gratitude to:

❖ All the ArtsReach family—the administrators and board members past and present, my fellow instructors, those who offered funding and other support, the educators who welcomed and collaborated with the program, the tribal officials who believed in its vision, the audiences who applauded the students' writings, the Native authors who honored them with publication in *Dancing with the Wind*, and most of all the ArtsReach students and families themselves

❖ Eva Martinez and Dora Manuel, who were indispensable in helping me locate the people whose voices are the content of this book

❖ Larry Evers, for his encouragement of the nascent project

❖ Mick Fedullo, Karen McIlroy, and Kelsey McIlroy for their astute readings of the book-in-progress

❖ Kitsune Books, for sharing my conviction that these unique lives and writings deserve to be published

# Contents

# Introduction

During the first public reading by the nonprofit ArtsReach, Native American children and adolescents paraded up to the podium, one by one, to deliver their original stories and poems in firm, clear voices. The little girls wore dresses, one of fringed leather. Their hair was done up. The boys dressed in jeans.

ArtsReach had completed its second year delivering writing programs to schools in the Yaqui and Tohono O'odham communities of southern Arizona. The reading was the 1989 Tucson Poetry Festival, the site a basement auditorium in the old YWCA. The children's shirts and dresses reflected off the scuffed, glossy black stage floor. Behind the podium a dangling movie screen swayed irrelevantly in the breeze from an evaporative cooler. After every story or poem the audience's applause echoed. Most were family members of the readers.

Many gifts passed from readers to listeners: a screaming wind that talked to the poet and helped her work, cattle stampeding through the sky, home-made tortillas. A first-grader asked, "How did rivers become? Did people make animals, or God?" One poet evoked his ancestors "racing with time, playing among the stars." Imagining the invention of mini-skirts, another reader proudly wore her own. A poet described the sacred Yaqui deer dancer—*maaso*—jumping "up and down, better, lighter." He knew the feeling because he danced *maaso* himself, in his village.

The MC was my younger self, resolutely uncharismatic as always.

I'm not relying on memory. I have the videotape.

In some cases, the self watching the video can foretell the future. I know that one tiny girl will grow up to read her poetry at the Smithsonian Institute's Museum of the American Indian, in

New York City, and her mother will serve on ArtsReach's Board of Directors. Another will write me letters in her looping, eight-year old handwriting, sprinkled with glitter. A stumpy, grinning boy will greet me years later during Yaqui Easter, handsome, towering, and I won't know who he is until he tells me his name. Another boy will marry and then commit a terrible crime. Husky-voiced Andrianna Escalante will become the first profile in this book.

Here I Am a Writer is about the writing life, not among professional authors, but Native American students who in most cases encountered creative writing through ArtsReach. Accidental writers, one could say, some only briefly writers—all left a published record, reproduced in this book. They since have grown into adulthood. They, and in some cases their family members, are the subjects of this retrospective. What courses have their lives taken since I met them a dozen or even twenty years ago? How lasting a mark did their writing episodes leave on them?

The relationship between art and life is endlessly, fascinatingly problematic. How "true" is any piece of writing, even if it purports to be non-fiction? Is there a truth more penetrating than mere factual truth? When does writing enhance the awareness of being alive, with all its complexities? When does it substitute for living, seducing the writer away from real experience? Should one live vividly to write vividly, or is the most valuable writing life the life of the mind?

The problem deepens in Native America, where written language is the tongue of the conqueror, where the heritage just beyond memory is the oral tradition. A profound literature of pre-conquest Native America survives, but it has been transcribed into print, when for centuries it was spoken and recited. The distinguished poet, fiction writer, and essayist Simon Ortiz views the impact of literacy itself upon his Acoma ancestors as catastrophic, overturning an entire way of relating to the world. So he writes, in English, with consummate literary skill, in his recent poem, "Memory, History, and the Present." Such are the paradoxes of the Native writer.

What inspires me in this work is the belief that people are at their best when writing, whatever the subject matter, because each poem or story honestly written is a focus of perception, imagination, memory, emotion, intellect, spirit, all in one. Nothing else so completely captures the flux of being.

For thousands of the young amateurs represented by the few profiles in *Here I Am a Writer*, writing began simply as a classroom assignment. In response to model poems and stories, given a few deliberately sketchy directions, they were asked to write something, and they did.

In some cases, that accomplishment was air to the drowning, food to the starving. An urban Tohono O'odham fifth-grader, mourning her cousin's death, commemorated her in a poem, hand-illustrated, that helped heal her family. In sixth grade this student stopped attending school—except for one week, the ArtsReach residency. How she learned of it I don't know, but all five days she bowed over her desk and wrote. (One of her stories was published.) Then she vanished again.

For others, like Andrianna Escalante, the ArtsReach residencies uncovered a secret self.

Or perhaps writing passed as no more than a happy curiosity. Jokingly, Eucario Mendez suspects he might have used his published output to prop up furniture.

Writing in a language foreign, even hostile, to their ancestors, all these students left their mark. If literature is meaning made beautiful through form and expressive power—regardless of any intrinsic loveliness, ugliness, humor, sadness—the students created literature.

Writing this introduction, I feel like that MC. I know you're here for the kids, reader, as you should be. But I must impose myself a bit, impart some requisite information, before we get to the program.

ArtsReach was founded by myself and two other rank novices, all white, in 1986. Mick Fedullo had taught poetry on the

Akimel O'odham (Pima) reservation since 1979, the same year I was hired as a writer-in-residence by the Arizona Commission on the Arts. My wife Karen had run the circulation departments for magazines, helped launch a pre-school, and trained early childhood educators.

As much as anything, I think we saw ArtsReach as an attempt to rectify glaring wrongs.

Whatever its other accomplishments, the Reagan administration was not a good time for programs serving education, minorities, or the arts, which faced annual budget threats and cuts. (President Reagan was unaware that Native Americans were U.S. citizens, as a speech overseas revealed.)

Even as Mick's students produced poems so revelatory that they were published in daily newspapers, from the nearby *Arizona Republic*, in Phoenix, to the *Frankfurter Rundschau*, in Germany, and read aloud to prestigious national conferences, the young Native authors remained generally ignored, often despised, even by their own classroom teachers. ("These kids can't write. And they would *never* stand up and read their work in public. They're too shy." And much, much worse. ) It was infuriating.

While educators, none of us three had special qualifications (whatever those might be) for serving Native communities. Twenty years have not dispelled the sensation of being out of my depth, facing the culture and experience of Native people. I continue to feel perpetually off-balance. I must enjoy that sensation.

Our cumulative expertise in managing and funding a non-profit corporation was zero.

Only beer, I'm afraid, gave us the audacity to presume we were the people to accomplish such a thing. One evening in 1986, our talk turned to Mick's students, their remarkable talents in the midst of an alien, imposed educational system. Sipping our brews in the living room of Mick's apartment, we decided Something Must Be Done. We were indignant. We were eloquent. We were visionary. (Or so it seemed.) And suddenly, we were ArtsReach, though we hadn't named it yet. What an irresistible idea, applying the arts-in-education model to these unheard Native voices; funders would simply throw money at it.

Yes. Well. ArtsReach lived out its first decade in Karen's and my home because it couldn't afford an office. Our financial status might be summed up in one image: Karen addressing a row of urinals, pleading for money, because a local business group happened to be meeting in a plumbing supply shop.

As to my cultural expertise, during my first residency with O'odham primary school students, I told a delightful Pima tale of how the rattlesnake got his fangs, only to learn that such stories, as well as the mention of rattlesnakes, were forbidden outside of winter. I immediately fell ill for two weeks, either from the spiritual transgression or my guilt.

Somehow, however, ArtsReach survived. During its first twenty years it engaged upwards of 10,000 students in the quest of imaginative writing. The largest number were Native, the others primarily Hispanic but also white, African-American, and Asian-American. Over a thousand have read their creations at the University of Arizona, the Yaqui and Tohono O'odham government complexes, the National Indian Education Association Conference, and numerous other venues. Yet more have been published in the ArtsReach annual, *Dancing with the Wind*. The list of Native authors who have volunteered as guest editors is astonishing. I must name them all: Sherman Alexie, Christina Castro, Debra Magpie Earling, Joy Harjo (twice), Danny Lopez, N. Scott Momaday, Irvin Morris, Darryl Noble, Simon Ortiz (twice), Leslie Marmon Silko, Luci Tapahonso, Laura Tohe, Franci Washburn, Darryl Babe Wilson, Ofelia Zepeda (twice).

Hundreds of teachers, administrators, tribal leaders, and others helped carry ArtsReach those twenty years. Nine different directors have served, and dozens of board members. Over twenty instructors have worked in the field, just under half of them Native.

ArtsReach never did master the fundraising game,

though. After constant financial struggles, it merged in 2007 with the Tucson Indian Center, where it continues as a TIC program.

"Diversity" may be a clichéd buzzword, but it's also responsible for the ArtsReach programs' enduring popularity.

The noted author Mao Zedong (*Little Red Book*) famously declared, "Let a hundred flowers bloom." Unfortunately, Mao is also remembered as a mass murderer, a caution against equating writing with virtue. Writing is just writing. While I consider creating stories and poems a near-holy act, capturing as does little else our individual essences and the adventure of being alive, it doesn't make us, the writers, saints.

But Mao's advice could apply to ArtsReach's hands-off attitude toward its guest instructors, all practicing writers, some renowned. Let them teach their own styles. ArtsReach never has imposed guidelines, much less a curriculum, upon them. Thus Mick Fedullo might win his students' love—and commitment to writing—by freaking them out with traditional stories such as "Cut-off Head," or rubber snakes and fake dog poop.

Darryl Babe Wilson supplied actual buckskin parchments for his students to write the final drafts of their autobiographies.

Three days into Simon Ortiz's residency at Baboquivari High, the language arts teacher, Mike Harty, called me, somewhat concerned. "He's just talking to them. They're not writing."

"Oh, well," I said helpfully. But Simon's trenchant, angry observations on the Native experience had provoked the classes as no one else could. The last two days, poems poured in, many written at home.

Danny Lopez, the late Tohono O'odham elder and storyteller, was prevented from teaching writing at all during one residency at the San Xavier mission school. The students demanded that he keep telling them stories, the oral literature of themselves as a people, which many never had heard.

But what really is the impact of such a program? Let's get real here, writer-guy: WHAT EFFECT DOES ARTSREACH HAVE ON TEST SCORES?

I'd prefer to ask, what effect does it have on the soul, whatever that might be?

But for decades I've considered that accountability question, which becomes ever more insistent as standardized testing dominates public education. From the beginning, I've believed that forging a meaningful connection, a sense of personal ownership, between students and writing *has* to benefit them academically. Students are more teachable, more attentive, more motivated, when they actually care about what they've written. They revise more willingly, which is when the most dramatic learning takes place—from content through the drab necessities of spelling and punctuation.

Assessing ArtsReach's direct impact on testing proficiency has been difficult, since that factor is inseparable from others, such as the day-to-day influence of the classroom teacher, or the vagaries of the scoring systems.

Occasionally, though, a natural laboratory does present itself. During the 1990's a school whose testing scores consistently had declined incorporated an ArtsReach teacher training program. Again school scores dipped—except in writing, where they spiked. Another school saw the number of third graders passing the AIMS, Arizona's standardized test, double from one year to the next when ArtsReach focused on personal narrative writing.

Of course I want students to score well. Their success in school, as well the careers of their teachers and administrators, most of them dedicated and capable, depend on it. I'm glad to help when asked. Recently I've devoted residency weeks to writing directions, comparing and contrasting, or second-grade persuasions. These are valid skills. But all too often, teachers are understandably afraid—the testing culture rules through fear—to risk precious instruction time on anything else. As if stories and poems are devoid of Ideas and Content, or lack Organization, or don't exhibit Voice, or are unconcerned with Sentence Fluency or Word Choice, or don't depend on Conventions. Creative writing teaches skills, too. *And students need it.* Their lives are full to bursting, with grief, joy, yearning, rage, fear. Where can that go? Into a test prompt commanding them to describe their classroom to an imaginary pen pal?

A daylong writing binge, riding that jangly adrenaline crest of the imagination, had broken my connection to the everyday, leaving me spent and dreamy. Darkness had long since fallen as I drove to the Old Pascua Yaqui village, where the silhouettes of worshippers played among the lights of food booths and the tiny, open chapel. Two uncanny beings crawled into its entrance. Though dressed as humans, torsos wrapped in blankets, one revealed the furred head and snarling teeth of a werewolf. On the other dead-white slab of face, black and red strokes formed a hideous scowl, while gigantic ears flared into delicate points, like a pig's. The back of my neck bristled, my spine tingled. *Big, weird animals were sneaking into the chapel!*

"Hey, Mr. Kit. Buy me a hot chocolate." A couple of kids shaking me down for snacks dispelled the trance, and its glimpse into another world.

The Yaqui (Hiaki, Yoeme) of southern Arizona are a rarity in U.S. Native history—refugees to this country, fleeing oppression elsewhere.

Settled originally along the Rio Yaqui in southern Sonora, Mexico, the Yaquis repelled Spanish military invasions but permitted Jesuit missionaries to introduce Roman Catholicism into their ancient religion. The Jesuits helped organize the eight major pueblos that still exist today near the city of Guaymas. When silver was discovered, the Spanish once again infiltrated Yaqui land. For the next two centuries the Yaquis, and their allies the Mayos, tried to drive them, and later the Mexicans, out. By the late 19th century, bitter warfare, massacre, enslavement, and outbreaks of smallpox forced waves of Yaquis to relocate.

Only since 1978 have the Yaquis been a federally recognized U.S. tribe. The Pascua Yaqui reservation is small, under

2,000 acres of desert southwest of Tucson. It often is referred to as New Pascua or New Village, in contrast to Old Pascua, tucked away in central Tucson. The Yaquis interviewed in this book grew up in Old Pascua, attending Richey School. Other communities in Arizona include Yoem Pueblo in Marana, northwest of Tucson; Barrio Libre in South Tucson; Guadalupe, southeast of Phoenix; Penjamo in Scottsdale; High Town in Chandler; and Somerton, near Yuma.

The Yaqui Easter ceremonies, Holy Week in particular, attract hundreds of spectators annually. While viewers are enthralled by the spectacle, the Lenten season, *cuaresma*, is a religious devotion that touches each Yaqui family. If not a direct participant, everyone has close relatives involved.

It's not hard to see what appeals to the public. Night by night, Christ's capture, crucifixion, and resurrection are transformed into a dramatic Yaqui ritual of good versus evil.

The *chapayekas*, members of the Fariseo religious society, cover their entire heads in homemade masks of demonic-looking animals, humans—from a Roman soldier to a Spanish conquistador to Richard Nixon—or even cartoon figures, such as a Teenage Mutant Ninja Turtle. While hilarious physical comedians, communicating only through gestures and pantomime, the *chapayekas* portray evil incarnate. Their sudden lunges scatter children with shrieks of laughter and real fear.

Their allies, the *Caballeros*, dressed in black, march stern and straight with wooden swords at their sides.

Arrayed against them are the Good. *Angelitas*, tiny children in starchy dresses and leafy crowns, fiercely whip the *chapayekas* with long twigs. *Matachinis* in floral headdresses of streaming colored paper wheel in formation, to the shaking of gourds and plaintive fiddle melodies.

*Pascolas* in goatish, hand-carved wooden masks shuffle intricate steps, rattling their cocoon anklets, around *maaso*, the Deer Dancer, who, with a deer head mounted on his own embodies the spirit of the animal itself.

To the observer, the festivities can be as dizzying as a runaway carousel, the *chapayekas* cavorting and clowning to one side, firing cap pistols; to the other, the Deer Dancer stalking to the throb of drums and Yaqui singing. Fireworks erupt. *Cantoras* wail Latin hymns. Bonfires blaze. Families clatter up and down aluminum bleachers. From the rows of food booths wafts the smoky aroma of fresh chili stew.

For all the extravagance of sensation, some of my favorite moments are the pensive ones, a solitary *chapayeka* removing his mask by firelight, a chat with a former student, 2 a.m., leaning against the root stump of a felled cottonwood.

At the climax of *cuaresma*, *Sábado de Gloria*, the dozens of *chapayekas* storm the chapel repeatedly. To the clanging alarm of bells, each wild rush is thwarted by the Good, including families inside, who hurl colored confetti, symbolic of flowers, or real flower petals. In Yaqui belief, flowers spring from the blood of Christ. Spectators join in, smacking open colorful *cascarones*, eggshells filled with confetti, which they fling at the *chapayekas* charging by. Whatever one's faith, the mix of exhilaration, peril, and sheer fun is intoxicating. This is no acting. The people are under assault by evil. You can see it in their grimaces, their fierce throws into the faces of their attackers.

Finally, the defeated *chapayekas* shed their masks and sticks into a fire, already glowing and crackling with a burning effigy of Judas. Once again their human selves, they run across the dirt plaza to rejoin the community, within the sanctuary of the chapel. This is the part that always catches at my throat. After forty days of ceremonies, they are exhausted. They have sweltered in the midday heat, under masks, blankets, and overcoats. Now they are running, when a fall, so I've heard, can portend ill luck, even death, during the coming year. Their faces are red, sweating. Then their godparents join them, running alongside, sheltering their heads with a blanket or coat, holding them up by the arms if need be. The chapel welcomes them inside.

The Tohono O'odham (formerly known as Papago) are widely believed to descend from the Hohokam, pre-Columbian engineers of vast irrigation systems in the Sonoran Desert. Their modern history alternates periods of peaceful coexistence with active resistance against the occupying powers.

Their first European contact probably was the Spanish wanderer Cabeza de Vaca, in the 16th century, but widespread interaction, through Jesuit missionaries, did not take place for another hundred years. While many O'odham congregated around the missions, accepting Christianity and European norms of civilization, at least four major revolts broke out between 1695 and 1776. After Arizona became U.S. territory, Anglo encroachment led to constant friction over land and water rights. The ultimate results were the reservations established in 1874 and 1917, and the Southern Arizona Water Rights Settlement Act of 1982, which resolved a lawsuit demanding restoration of O'odham water lost to urban development.

The Tohono O'odham Nation is vast, 2.8 million acres, the second-largest reservation in the United States, but sparsely populated. Of the approximately 24,000 Tohono O'odham—translated as Desert People—some 11,000 live within its boundaries. The reservation is composed of eleven districts, including two tiny, separate communities far to the north. The San Xavier District, bordering Tucson, is home to both the gleaming, whitewashed mission of the same name, originally built by the O'odham under Father Eusebio Kino, and the Desert Diamond Casino.

The main reservation, consisting of eight districts, begins about twenty miles west of Tucson. Its southern boundary shares the frontier with Mexico, a source of considerable grief. Already the border divides ancestral O'odham lands and people from each other. Since 9/11, the Department of Homeland Security has tightened controls, while the Secure Fence Act of 2006 threatens more permanent barriers. Meanwhile, immigrant and drug smuggling overwhelms traditional O'odham hospitality with violence, trash, and the desecration of sacred sites; the stepped-up Border Patrol response scars the land and ruins fences, releasing cattle to menace the high-speed roadways. The reservation, with its miles of empty desert, in some areas can take on the appearance of a war zone, law enforcement SUVs roaring every which way. A friend's granddaughter lost her father, run over and killed by the Border Patrol.

I've been stopped myself, as a "suspicious vehicle," by an O'odham cop.

"How am I suspicious?" I asked.

"You're white," he replied, with disarming frankness.

Still, the landscape enchants with its rugged mountains and profusion of starkly beautiful vegetation, much of it spiny. The spray of dry thorned sticks known as ocotillo leafs out green, tipped by red blossoms, after a soaking rain. The stately saguaro, with its arms outstretched or writhing, is a person, according to an O'odham story. Long ago, they say, a mother, obsessed with *toka*, the traditional stick game resembling field hockey and played by women, neglected her daughter. The child buried herself in the earth, emerging as a *ha:san* (saguaro), giving its red *bahidaj* fruit to the people.

The mountain *Waw Giwulk* (corrupted to "Baboquivari") is the spiritual center of the Tohono O'odham. Visible for miles in every direction, the distinctive granite dome is home to I'itoi, the Man in the Maze prominent in O'odham basketry and jewelry. And elsewhere, apparently; I don't know how to explain the Man in the Maze pin I encountered at a street market in Florence, Italy.

The maze often is interpreted as the journey of life, or also, as an O'odham woman once told me, a metaphor for traditional storytelling. All stories are one story, she said, with each being a part of the maze. It's like a spider's web: any part that is struck, the rest vibrates to it.

The O'odham *Himdag*, or traditional way, is woven into the cycle of the seasons. In the past, many families kept winter and summer homes. In winter, they hunted in the mountains. During summer, they farmed the desert in the *ak chin* method, capturing rainwater to irrigate tepary beans, squash, corn, and melons. At the proper times they gathered cholla buds and mesquite beans. After displaying its creamy white blossoms, the saguaro produced the *bahidaj* for eating and ceremonial wine. Traditional storytelling is confined to the winter months. *Piasts*, celebrations, occur throughout the year, and may be the occasion for dancing *waila*, AKA chicken scratch. *Waila* bands play an O'odham-flavored hybrid of Europan polka and Mexican *norteño*. To be caught up in the spinning galaxy of whirling couples, dust rising in a haze from scuffling feet, is both grounding and otherworldly to the outsider.

Nowadays you'll hear just as much rap, reggae, and hard, hard rock.

The tribal radio station, KOHN, beams a mix of music and commentary, some of it in O'odham, across as much of the rez as its low wattage will allow. Leaving the reservation, I know that once I'm alongside Kitt Peak the reception will fade, contesting with an evangelical Christian station. For miles the two will struggle for airspace equally, a burst of sax and accordion alternating with drawl-tinged exhortations to follow Jesus.

Both Yaquis and Tohono O'odham prepare really delicious food, including the astronomically caloric frybread, or popover, often topped with honey, or red or green chili. Either color is fresh, roasted green or stewed red, bits of pod floating in it—no canned or powdered. The tortillas—*cemait* in O'odham—are slightly elastic, moist, dotted with black dots from toasting. They don't dry out, brittle. Probably loaded with lard. Some of the best food I've ever eaten is from the parking lot in Sells, the main Tohono O'odham town, or booths at the Yaqui Easter ceremonies.

And both Yaqui and Tohono O'odham suffer the plagues of other tribes, high unemployment and alcoholism, early death from disease, violence, auto accidents, suicide, the looming shadow of tragedy.

To survive, my Native friends have attained the toughness

and beauty of the hardy desert plants.

My plan for *Here I Am a Writer* was to interview former students, then link those oral histories between their old writings and new pieces. Re-connecting them to the writing habit did not always prove easy, however, and whenever I risked becoming a complete pest I dropped that notion. I'm grateful for the time my collaborators gave me. I deeply appreciate their patience and kindness. It was a joy meeting with them again.

Once again I savor memories.

At the conclusion of that inaugural ArtsReach reading, Karen and I gathered up the students from the YWCA basement and took them out for pizza. They chatted excitedly, autographing each other's ArtsReach books. Yaqui and O'odham, tribes living only an hour apart—many had not heard of the other before that event, and now they shared an authors' signing party.

Pride. The pride in each reader's face, looking up to receive applause. The pride in parents' voices over the phone, hearing that their son or daughter had been chosen to read or publish. "She was chosen out of all those kids?" Or, "He's not in trouble?"

There are those luminous instants when students "get it"—when suddenly they grasp the possibilities in their drafts and can't wait to plunge back into their own material. The impact shows through even the mundane evaluation forms: "I learned to give more attention to the world and that the world around us is really beautiful." As a third-grader reminds us, "It is hard work when you get to understand the meaning of writing."

Above all, I think, is the wonder at what the students have made. Over lunch, at times, I'll spread the handwritten manuscripts around my plate, occasionally spattering them with salsa, as I nod at an inventive passage, laugh, or sit back in awe. Occasionally I must read them aloud, on the spot, to whatever stranger might be nearby.

Observing, a waitress once asked what I do. I told her.

"That sounds like fun," she said. "You're lucky."

Yes, I am.

I've chosen the particular lives for this book because they or their body of work intrigued and moved me. In most but not all cases I sought out the people I had known best because I thought they were most likely to talk to me. So either I had intense personal memories of them, as with Marisa Yucupicio, who used to babysit my child, or I'd shared contact with them over many years, as with Patrick Lewis-Jose. Eucario Mendez is an exception; I taught in his sixth grade class a week or two and scarcely saw him again until knocking at his door eighteen years after. Yet I've showed off his story, "Mr. John," to so many classrooms and workshops that it lives in my head.

Many brilliant and valued students are not represented here, due, for the most part, to circumstance: I hooked up with other people first. And once I did, I found that the process of interviewing them thoroughly, enough to hope I'd grasped at least some partial truth, was long. I learned that others' lives do not fit into my timetable. Crises intervened, theirs and mine. I realized that by the time I interviewed all those I would like, the first group would be drawing Social Security.

More Tohono O'odham than Yaqui appear, with more extensive portfolios. Again, circumstance. I've accompanied several groups of O'odham through ascending grade levels in the Indian Oasis-Baboquivari School District. Wenona Ortegas and Patrick Lewis-Jose, for instance, were sixth graders together, joined in seventh by Josie Frye. I visited their class every year until they graduated in 1997. In contrast, the Old Pascua Yaqui students, after attending their neighborhood Richey School, disperse throughout the enormous Tucson Unified School District, where ArtsReach and I lose track of them.

No writer in this collection has gone pro, and perhaps none will, though some already use writing in their professions. Few view themselves as artists. At certain times in their lives, when given the opportunity, all found the artist within them,

embraced it, or moved on, leaving behind these poems and stories for us. For at least that time they could say, as did Josie Frye, who ended her story "Eclipse and Commode" with these words…
"Here I am a writer."

—*Lorianne Narcho*

# ANDRIANNA ESCALANTE

Andrianna "Ande" Escalante was born and raised in the Old Pascua neighborhood, where she still lives. She is a member of the Yaqui tribe.

# Yaqui Words

*Choki:* This is the star
that goes on the flag.
It is like a ring
that shines
in the sun.

*Wo'i:* I see a coyote dancing
to the night music
like a desert mesquite tree
when the
wind blows.

*Taa'a:* I can see the sun.
It is our father.
It is like a yellow bird
when it is flying smoothly
through the air.

*—Ande Escalante, 5ᵗʰ Grade*

# In the Desert

I start walking and
as I walk I look
into the desert.
Remembering  my
late father as we
used to walk in
the desert.
I look to the
mountains where the
sun has disappeared.
Tears come falling down.
I can still
remember him.

*—Ande Escalante, 6ᵗʰ Grade*

# Rose Is a Cherry Candy

Rose is a cherry candy. I smelled the rose, and it was sweet. I felt it, and it was breaking on the palm of my hand. And when I was picking that rose, it was like a good, slow heartbeat was in me.

*—Ande Escalante, 6ᵗʰ Grade*

# The Cowboy

One night my mom was driving to my house. That was when I used to live in New Village, and when my dad was still alive.

Well, my mom was driving, and she was alone. She was getting off the freeway, and she saw this one cowboy dressed in black. The cowboy waved at my mom, so my mom waved back. While she was driving, she felt a cold feeling inside of her. It was midnight, and there was no light, and it was dark where she was driving.

When she got home, she couldn't walk. She called my dad, and my dad helped my mom in the house. My mom told my dad that she felt cold. She made the sign of the cross like she always did, and went to sleep. That coldness went away when she made the sign of the cross.

When she woke up, she told my dad what had happened. My dad said that cowboy was a ghost and she shouldn't have waved to him. That's why the coldness was in her. My dad said it was a good thing she made the sign of the cross. My mom got scared.

That day, my parents went for us at my grandma's, and told my grandma and us what happened. We got scared.

This happened on Valencia Road. This was true.

*—Ande Escalante, 6th Grade*

◎  ◎  ◎  ◎  ◎  ◎

There's danger, as one person loses contact with another, of that other becoming an emblem. After Andrianna (Ande) Escalante left Richey Elementary in 1989, the less I actually spoke with her, the more I conceived of her as the ArtsReach Poster Child. Her story was gritty, down-to-earth: somebody who had struggled toward success, sometimes faltering, who while not a professional writer had integrated writing as a vital part of her life.

True, as far as it goes, which, as with any shorthand attempt to grasp another human being, is not very far.

Ande was my first interview in this series, my first collision with its realities. My first acknowledgement was that, while my project was central to me, to my subjects I was very peripheral, alien, and a bit of a nuisance. Months elapsed between my first interview with Ande and the second.

Of course, there is the obvious cultural gulf between an Anglo writer/educator and indigenous people. For instance, Ande relaxes back into her worn, comfortable couch, legs crossed, chuckling as she describes her deceased father tattling on her—in her mother's dreams. It's as matter-of-fact as if he were phoning in by cell; the spiritual dimension of dreams—of everything, for that matter—is a given. I, meanwhile, try to nod comprehendingly while my thrilled mind reels.

We are of different generations, as well, though this may matter less to young Natives, who tend to live intimately by their older relatives.

Most importantly, there's the fact of real life overwhelming one's superficial understandings and preconceptions.

For starters, the shy kid with the half-smile and sad eyes has become a highly functioning adult, fielding phone calls and children's demands without breaking her narrative thread while we talk, in the midst of her immaculate home—even the front yard looks swept. It's summer, 2006, a swamp cooler humming away the heat.

Ande was one of ArtsReach's first students. "To be honest, I didn't know anything about poetry or writing until then," she says. "At first, being a kid, it's like 'agggh, we have to write.' But then it's a way of bringing emotions out, emotions that you can't show. It had a lot to do with my dad. It helped me."

Her father, John Escalante, recently had died, the pivotal event of her young life. Twenty years later, Ande's face goes faraway. "I used to cry to stay out there with him in New Pascua. There was nothing there but the stars. That night he was insistent to take us, me and my sister, but I decided to stay behind. My dad said, 'Come on, come on, let's go.' I said, 'No no no no.' I guess I knew he was going to pass on. I remember holding myself on my knees and just rocking myself. 'Don't pass away. Don't pass away.'" Her voice chants the words.

"He'd been having chest pains. In the morning he was getting ready to go to work, and he had a massive heart attack. He was forty-two."

Like many writers, Ande did not excel in school. In fact, she had been retained once by the time she won a statewide poetry contest in fifth grade. Her winning entry, "Yaqui Words," composed in a class with ArtsReach co-founder Mick Fedullo, delivers sweeping, daring imagery with a few simple phrases. A star becomes a ring, a coyote is a swaying tree, and the sun soars as a bird. The poem is visionary, in an everyday way.

With the poem "In the Desert," Ande grieved openly. But even indirectly, she says, "That cowboy one, thinking about my dad, my mom going home and my dad being there, it was a way of helping me get through."

The lyricism of "Rose Is a Cherry Candy," on the other hand, is mysteriously evocative, enigmatic. "There's a different person inside of me," Ande explains. "That person who wrote."

It's a theme we'll return to, and a discovery about Ande,

her many selves.

I can't help thinking about another favorite, gifted student, Wenona Ortegas, who also lost her father at an early age, wrote about him obsessively, and, it seemed to me, couldn't survive his loss. She died in a car crash at the age of twenty-eight.

I ask Ande what pulled her through.

"My dad was still here."

I wait.

"He would come into my mom's dreams and tell her what I was up to. My mom would ask me, 'What were you up to last night?'

"I said, 'Nothing.'

"She said, 'No you were doing…' And it was true." Ande laughs heartily. "She'd say, 'No, your dad said this and that. Don't think you're out there alone because he's watching you.'"

In fact, Ande confesses, shortly after entering high school, she had become a *traviesa*—a scamp or wrongdoer—dabbling in *la vida loca.*

Ande a gangbanger?

"I did get into the gangs and stuff. I guess I wanted to fit in." She'd known the gangsters all her life, neighborhood teenagers like her cousin, Martín Acuña. "I didn't want to be that way." Her mother, Linda, helped. "She let us experience consequences for ourselves. I think she knew I was going to get out of it. That was just a phase I was going through."

And there was Ande's dad. "Maybe that's what kept me kind of in line, why I didn't get too much into the gang. Because I knew my dad was watching over me."

What did Ande learn from gangs? "Nothing," she answers curtly.

Ande would find peace and resolution around her father's death, too, though she would have to wait another ten years or more. While her mother met him in sleep, Ande didn't dream of him at all. "Not once, ever," she says. "Not once had I heard him, not once had I seen him in my dreams. Two years ago, three years ago, I told my mom, 'My dad doesn't care about us any more like in the past, when he used to say he was watching over us. Maybe there's other things he needs to do.'

"And then I dreamed that we went to go visit him, me and my mom, at his gravesite. The dirt is brown, and he has a cross just like this one." (She gestures toward the front yard.) "Then it all was totally white. Something from out of nowhere says, 'Knock over there. We're going to open the door for you.' I'm like, what? We go around the gravesite, on that side, me and my mom, and I'm just knocking into air. Into nothing. My mom says, 'Come on, let's go, there's nobody there.' So we turn around and start walking, and all of a sudden the other side opens. It was weird. A ray of light comes out. My little cousin comes out—he passed away when he was five, he had cerebral palsy—he comes out running, running, running around us. My dad came out. My mom got him by the head and hugged him and rocked him like she hadn't seen him in forever.

"My dream was a way of letting me know that my dad is O.K., and he's up in Heaven now. When children pass away, they go straight up to heaven. That's what we believe in. For the rest of us, all those prayers that we said for him helped him to get up to Heaven."

In high school, Ande tried out the *traviesa* persona, found it didn't fit. "I knew I was doing wrong, but inside I was still the artsy type. That person was hiding inside me, the person who wanted to keep dancing, poetry, art." Her godmother gave her a sketchbook, which she partially filled with drawings "from the time that I got grounded and I was bored at home," she laughs. She opens the binder now to sketches of a shimmering cross, soulfully haunted adolescent faces.

Failing during her senior year, Ande transferred to an alternative high school, determined to graduate. A month after earning her diploma, she became pregnant. "Once my son was born, I changed and became the person who I wanted to be. I think I became what I am because my mom molded me."

Eight months after the birth, she was hired by Pascua Yaqui Head Start, where she continues to teach. She and the father of their three boys, Alvino Godoy, have been together for fifteen years. Their house in the Old Pascua neighborhood, modest and well-ordered, carries a particular "sentimental" value for her.

"I helped build this house from the ground up," Ande says proudly. "They blessed the ground, we did the groundbreaking. They put the foundation in. We helped raise the walls, put together the frames, stucco, painting. The *chapayekas* came to bless the house, wearing masks. It was *cuaresma* [the Lenten season]." The *chapayekas* play a complex role: while portraying evil, they also are sacred figures in a sacred ceremony. Their antics can be as comic as they are frightening.

Since her earliest memories, Ande has embraced her culture. As a toddler, she would play *chapayekas* with other neighborhood kids. Wearing discarded 12-pack boxes on their heads—"just that, and Pampers"—the tiny mimics marched around the yard banging sticks together, playing a role handed down for centuries. At age three, an *angelita* in a starchy, gauzy dress, Ande helped defend the church against those *chapayekas* and their allies. Now she is a *cantora*, singing prayers, often in Latin, during *cuaresma* and other sacred occasions.

"As Natives," Ande says, "we're passionate about our families, our values, and our culture."

At Head Start, "I'm trying to build a foundation for the students' lives," she continues. "Teaching them what to expect. Being social. Being there for them."

While preparing students for kindergarten, the Head Start program also instructs in Yaqui culture and simple language. Ande herself understands more Yaqui than she speaks, while her grandmother was fluent, a common, sad development among Native American generations. "They have Yaqui language classes for adults now. And that's what I want to do, then go teach the guys what I know. There's that other part of me that wants to do more and more, give more."

She also provides an annual program for neighborhood children, at the church. "In a way I'm a role model for these little guys. They see me praying and doing *cantora* and getting involved with schools. I try to be positive with them.

"The students that I first had as a co-teacher are going into high school already. One or two still call me 'teacher.' Wow. That's how they see me."

I remind Ande of her two childhood ambitions, to be a poet and a dentist. We laugh about "the oral tradition."

Ande's life would be full enough embodying all these aspects of a modern yet traditional Yaqui woman—mother, partner, homeowner, educator, a person who inhabits the spiritual realm through community ritual and private dreaming. With flowing black hair to her waist, rounded face and body, serene demeanor and generous smile, she inspires trust, belief.

Yet there remains one self not entirely integrated.

About her writing, Ande admits, "I haven't really kept it going, but I know it's inside me. I feel it. It's in a little box, wanting to come out."

For a moment I glimpse the conflict that all artists face, between their adult responsibilities to others and that demanding inner voice. "I want to keep writing. I want to keep drawing. I want to play the guitar. They ask me if I want to dance, and I say, oh yeah, but I can't because I want to spend time with the kids. I'd like to go to a gallery, but there's no one to go with me. I've never really talked about the way I am inside. I know that person better than the other part of me."

What she can do is share the gift with others. "My students at school like writing. Not writing, but dictating." She helps them incorporate stories into other projects, such as a recent study of insects. "They made this big insect world. They used stamps and colored it and whatnot. They came up with a story about what they'd made, their creation. Everyone had their own story of what's going on in the picture.

"I'm giving it to these guys. I'm passing it on to them."

When her oldest son, Alvino, read his writing at a school talent show, "It hit me. Oh my God, this is what I was doing when I was his age. I was listening to him, just crying."

Our second visit, a chilly January afternoon, under an overcast sky with swirling winds, Ande sits me on the front porch with a glass of hot cinnamon tea. The front yard is dominated by a rugged cross formed of mesquite logs, a present from Ande's uncle. At the moment it is draped with a homemade drum and *chapayeka* masks, soon plucked off by a parade of children. While we two adults chat, Ande's three sons, Alvino, Adrian, and Abram, two nephews, and a niece, march about us wearing the paper masks, one a plastic SWAT helmet, beating the drum in the age-old *chapayeka* cadence as Ande did decades ago. "The spirit never dies," she says.

"I can hardly be indoors," Ande has told me. Nature, which inspired much of her early writing, "is something that is still inside me. I like stargazing. Especially when the wind's blowing, I'm like, ohhhh." So she has chosen this setting for her new poem.

As she jots rapidly, her boys ask, "What is she doing?"

Finished, she remarks, "The way I write is different from the way I talk. Way different. It's like a different person."

The writing self has chosen the domestic self, an ode to her home, but with Ande's characteristically bold, idiosyncratic details peeking through.

I've wondered if Ande sees the writer as linked to the dreamer, or the spiritual person, but she says absolutely not. "The writing person is separate from the others. I go into a daze, or something like that. I start thinking of things.

"There are a lot of people inside me that I can probably name."

Ande does have a new dream.

"I hardly ever dream. I only dream when something is

telling me something. I dream because someone is warning me, or it's warning my family, just to keep a watch. Or if I haven't seen somebody for a long time, I dream about them and I know that I'm going to see them a few days later, or the next day. In my other dream, just recently, I was flying. In our custom, when you dream about flying, you have a gift. I'm still trying to figure out what gift it is." She laughs.

The neighborhood where Ande and her parents grew up has changed. "It's kind of funny how my mom used to say, 'It's not how it used to be back then.' Now I'm saying that to my kids. When I was Alvino Jr.'s age, I used to cross the street and play. Now I can't let my kids do that, only because of the shootings that have been going around. When I was growing up, there wasn't anything like that. There were fights. Never any shootings whatsoever."

But her dream seems purely exhilarating. "I would just run and take off, soaring, above the whole neighborhood. I could see everything. I saw the roofs. I was flying around at night. It was great. When I got up, I had it in my mind. I knew I'd had a dream, but I also felt like I could really take off. I really wanted to run and go up. I'm still trying to figure out what that means. If I did, I could put that gift to use now."

My lazy instinct was not incorrect: Ande *is* a poster child for ArtsReach. At moments, writing has intersected with her life to help her discover herself, and to reveal a person of infinite value. And the same is true for hundreds, for thousands, of other ArtsReach students whom I never will know even this much, from what a few hours' talking can teach me. How insubstantial our impressions of others, like footsteps on the moon!

## *In Kari*—My House

Comfort home, how you stand
with your warm leathered fur
to keep us warm
the windows made
of crystals and clouds
to cover as a roof.
Comfort home, how you
make everyone welcomed
with your seats of happiness.
When we sit, a smile appears instead
of frowns. When we eat
and drink, there is laughter,
giggles, and joy.
Your light within, how your light glistens
throughout the home with love,
the welcome, the warmth you bring.
Friends, if perchance you
feel a bit of sadness in your life,
whatever it may be, I invite you
to come into
my comfort home.

*—Ande Escalante, 2007*

—*Robert Arredondo*

# MARTÍN ACUÑA

Martín Acuña is a member of the Yaqui tribe. His home is in the Old Pascua neighborhood.

# Holes

If I had holes in my shoes, it would be a problem. If I were to step on a nail and my toe was sticking out, it would poke me and it would bleed, or a mouse could come by and suck my toe.

I think I will put paper bags over my toes. It worked!

*—Martín Acuña, 3rd Grade*

# Cold Breeze

I feel the cold
breeze blowing in
my face as I am
sitting on a rock
way up in the sky,
as I see God.

*—Martín Acuña, 5ᵗʰ Grade*

# Her Face

I see my nana in the kitchen making
tortillas with the blinds open and the sun shining
on the floor. Then her face is like a plum
as sweat drips down her face.

*—Martín Acuña, 6ᵗʰ Grade*

◎  ◎  ◎  ◎  ◎  ◎

Martín Acuña creates an impression. I remember him in elementary school, possibly third grade, entering the classroom flushed and sweating from recess. At least I think I do. Or maybe I'm conflating the actual memory with Martín's poem "Her Face," his nana ruddy and dripping like ripe fruit. Or maybe I retain another memory, Martín rampaging through the restroom and halls of a Tucson mall, dashing madly away from my wife while she tried to compose him for an ArtsReach reading.

Whatever the actual source, Martín's abiding presence for me is this hot, damp face. Heat, for his guiding and misguiding passions. And if we all understand "dry" as implying restraints to emotion, behavior, and taste, then Martín is "wet." There's wetness in his dark eyes and wide lips, in a furtive, elusive way of carrying himself, as water finds its way through unseen recesses.

Martín was the school *travieso*—troublemaker—not the only one, but the most notorious and popular. Some of that mischief sneaks through his story "Holes," featuring the toe-sucking mouse. One was alternately charmed and exasperated by him; his misbehavior had the knack of inciting others.

With his poem "Cool Breeze," I first glimpsed Martín's spiritual fervor, a dimension properly opaque to non-Yaquis. While still a schoolboy, he was dancing the ceremonial *pahko*. As a *pascola*, he portrayed the masked, sacred clowns who accompany the *maaso*, the Deer Dancer. At times Martín donned the deer head and danced *maaso* himself, becoming in those moments the "main guy," as he modestly acknowledges, in the pure, mythic realm of *Sea Ania*, the Flower World.

In dancing the life and death of the deer, the *maaso* embodies holy sacrifice and rebirth. For outsiders, the figure shocks us out of the everyday into the mysterious. Spurred on by

insistent wooden raspers, booming gourd water-drum, and the
wild tremblings of a wooden flute, the bare-chested dancer eerily
mimics the movements of the animal. The deer head atop his own
transfixes the viewer, poised, gazing, facing the hunter. Churning,
the hands twirl maracas that echo the deer's heartbeat while the
feet, clad in rattling cocoons, prance with an ethereal power and
delicacy.

During *cuaresma*, the Lenten and Easter ceremonies, the
deer dancer helps repel the masked *chapayekas* in their assaults on
the chapel.

Meanwhile, Martín admits, "when I was dancing deer
dancer, after that I'd be out in the streets." After "claiming" in fifth
grade, he ran with both Crips and Bloods. He threatened to "cap"
his sixth grade teacher with a 9 mm. pistol.

"Everybody says, how could you do this and then do
this?" Martín laughs. "Everyone was saying, you're a different
person here, and here. We don't know you."

We're talking in the apartment Martín shares with his
longtime love, Marisa Yucupicio, his daughter Iliana, and his son
Martín, Jr., though at the moment his family is elsewhere. Martín
is completely spent. Head bowed, ponytail limp against his neck,
a couple of inches shorter than my five-eight, he spoons ramen.
Though heavily tattooed, he doesn't look like Old Pascua's most
infamous gangbanger.

Martín has been laying masonry for the Pascua Yaqui
Tribe's senior center. When he works, he works hard. Problem is,
when he doesn't work, "I still mess up, you know. No, not gang
stuff any more, I just go out and drink. But sometimes, yeah,
there's always going to be someone out there...."

Rumored to be a drive-by shooter, Martín himself has
been shot several times. Between him and Marisa, the testimony
can be a bit fuzzy. Maybe four times? Three?

In fact, I feel fortunate to be speaking with him. Initially
we'd scheduled the interview two days earlier, but then he recalled
he had a hearing in Phoenix. "How about a couple of days later?  If

I'm not in jail," he'd said cheerfully, over the phone. Finding him at home, then, seemed a good sign.

Not necessarily. "I didn't show up in Phoenix," he explains. "I think I'll be all right. They probably put a warrant out, but it's nothing bad."

He understands perfectly the stark reality that holding on to the woman he loves, his children, stability, requires occupying himself—even exhausting himself—with labor. "Just this past weekend, after staying away two months, I decided to drink. That's just me, I guess. I can change it if I want to. It's just hard like—it keeps calling me back." His voice subsides to a mumble, nearly inaudible.

Leafing through his old ArtsReach writings, and Marisa's, seems to cheer him up. "It's amazing how we kids come up with these ideas. We're running around there, not thinking about anything, and we come in and sit down and start writing." He remembers reading his poems at the University of Arizona, and also dodging my wife at the mall. He finds that hilarious.

About Marisa, he says, "She's just the same. She has a good sense of how to put words together. She still does, helping me. Let's say I have to write something for the judge, or even with the kids, how to word it out." The puzzle to onlookers, including both the school and Old Pascua communities, has been the abiding match between Martín and the sunny, studious, virtuous, even-tempered Marisa Yucupicio.

Though stormy, interrupted by breakups and Martín's three years in jail, the relationship has endured, to this point, for sixteen years. The domestic apartment setting features a Yaqui touch—children's toys, a *pascola* mask dangling from a baseball trophy.

Martín readily acknowledges the attraction of opposites. "That's what everybody says!" Marisa remains the "good girl. She never got involved with gangs, not even a little bit. She stayed out of it. She kept me out of trouble back then, some—even now. Takes care of me when I'm messing. I don't know how to explain it. I love her, I love her."

His prison term tested that love. After jumping intensive probation, going on the run, he was captured, then imprisoned in Winslow, maximum security, from 2002-2005.

"I survived just by being myself," Martín says. "In there is a different world. Just the way you carry yourself. All you've got there is your word. Stick with your own people and you'll be alright. Every day you've got to be on your toes, can't turn your back on nobody, you know? If you do, if you let your guard down, you get killed.

"Marisa and the kids used to go see me. It was hard to see them leave. But mostly how I did my time was not think about them. I knew they were coming at certain times, but other than that I didn't worry about what was going on out here. Otherwise I'd start thinking about them. The first three months it was like, man, my kids, it was driving me crazy. I said, I'll block it out, forget about out there. If they write, they write. It was good that I had her. Couldn't do without her."

Dealing with Martín is a strange disconnect, for me and others, including his former teachers, not to mention his long-time partner. Though we know he's committed brutal crimes and terrible offenses against those who love him, we can't help rooting for him, his engaging charm, playfulness. At the height of his gangbanging, I remember him and his homies leaping on my car as I drove through Old Pascua, hammering on the hood, grinning faces pressed against the windshield. The joke was in equal parts menacing and affectionate. What may lift Martín to the level of tragic figure, if anything does, is his unflinching self-awareness. He makes no pretenses, no excuses.

"Marisa, it hurts her," he says. "So I'm trying to do what's right. I got a job. Sometimes that's not enough."

When I mention that I've taught his "Cool Breeze" to classrooms, as a model for visionary poetry, Martín starts up from the ramen bowl in surprise, moved. "That's a good feeling that you use my work."

He's willing to write a new piece, though he wants help with possible ideas. Discussing the difference between "beauty" and "prettiness" seems to excite him, particularly the notion that beauty could incorporate ugliness.

"Yeah, yeah. I'll give it a try. I'll tell Marisa."

That's the last I saw Martín. For months he took construction jobs out of town that, along with the commute, left him too fatigued to continue our interview.

His new writing folder remained empty until two years later, when I received a letter, along with a handwritten piece roughly self-edited with cross-outs. It follows.

The return address was a prison unit in Buckeye, Arizona. But that's another story, the next one.

# 2 People in One Body

As I look in this mirror I see one person.
A person with a good heart that could
be loving, trusted, even looked up to.
Only family knows this person that is loving,
caring, and trusted. Most of his friends don't
know this person. They see the other person.
As I look again in the mirror I see the other
person, the one that has no heart, that
doesn't care about others, the person that only cares
for himself. The one they look up to for the wrong
reasons. The person that will hurt you in any way.

*—Martín Acuña, 2008*

—*Bernadette Pablo*

# MARISA YUCUPICIO

Marisa Yucupicio is a member of the Yaqui tribe. She lives in the Old Pascua neighborhood, where she was born.

# The Frog Who Could Never Catch Flies

Long ago there was a frog who had a very short tongue. He was dark green and very shiny. Every day he would sit on a stone and be very hot and bored. The frog was always bored because he never had friends. The other frogs didn't like him because he could never catch flies. He always felt hungry, because flies passed by him like the wind. Because he had such a short tongue, he could not catch them.

He was hopping along one day, very hungry, when he met a talking bush right in the middle of the desert. This bush was very green and healthy and it had a beautiful fragrance. Her flowers smelled so good and her leaves were so soft and smooth. Suddenly the talking bush said, "I will grant you one wish." The frog was so excited he didn't know what to say. Then finally the frog said, "I wish so much that you would give me a long tongue." The talking bush said, "I will put this stick in your mouth. It will be perfect for a tongue, and don't worry how it tastes. You will get used to it."

Now that the frog had his long tongue, flies still thought it was a short tongue. Unafraid, they passed by him so slowly, and by the end of the day the frog had a full stomach. At night in order to fall asleep he would sing to himself. His songs were about thanking the talking bush and about flies.

—*Marisa Yucupicio, 5th Grade*

# House of Water and Feathers

In my house the walls are beautiful white, pouring waterfalls. I take a shower there. The floor is made of the Mississippi River. It flows very beautiful. I use that as my swimming pool. My furniture is made out of surfboards. I use those because I surf on my floor, and because when I sleep the water rocks me.

The roof is made of bread. Sometimes when I run out of food, I nibble on it. The beams are made of lettuce. I eat that all the time. The doors are made of spaghetti noodles. I always have to go to the store to buy more 'cause I always end up eating them.

The lights are made of fireflies. I have a lot of them at night so I can see where I'm going.

My porch is made of parrot feathers. I like to feel the porch because it's very soft.

The whole yard around my beautiful house is a big green jungle, floating on the floor, which is water. There are all kinds of animals. They are my pets. Every day I go outside in my jungle and look at my animals playing around, talking with rough and squeaky voices. I see birds flying all over the place above my head.

I hear the sounds they make when they talk, play, and fight. When they talk, you just hear them very quietly, but you can't understand them. When they play, they make squeaking noises, 'cause they yell. When the animals fight, they grunt in a loud noise.

Right in the middle of my jungle there is a clearing where I go every day to take my nap. Sometimes I wander off into the jungle and get lost. But I'm lucky, because the animals find me, and they lead me back.

*—Marisa Yucupicio, 6th Grade*

◎  ◎  ◎  ◎  ◎  ◎

At a time when classmates were beginning stories with lines such as, "I have seen a lot of death," Marisa Yucupicio wrote about a frog achieving its heart's desire, and a magical imaginary home in which the Mississippi River rocked her to sleep and wild beasts always guided her to safety.

"When I read these, I see how happy I was," Marisa says. "When I talk to other kids, compared to Martín and stuff he went through, it was never that way with me. I loved school. I loved going every day." At times Marisa can seem almost perplexed by her steadfast high spirits and positive outlook. Or that others don't share them.

After all, beyond even the ongoing *telenovela* with Martín, she's experienced her own parents' divorce, her sister's struggles with drug addiction. But, "back when I was growing up, if it was happening my mom hid it from us so well. I was really happy." And her sister "is a really good person. She's just not responsible when it comes to her choices.

"A lot of people in the neighborhood are like Martín. They get high and drink. They say, 'You think you're better than me.' But that's not it. I just don't care about it."

About five months after I spoke with Martín, Marisa has moved out, perhaps for good this time. She shares a house at the edge of Old Pascua, up against the railroad tracks, with her mother and the two children, Iliana, entering sixth grade, and Martín Jr., going into second. Despite intermittent train rumblings and piercing whistles, the house is neat and cozy, centered around an enormous stone fireplace and hearth.

The Marisa of 1988-89 smiled wide and often, big glasses accentuating her wide-eyed alertness. She still does, and they still do. Then she was an unabashed student achiever. Now she is being groomed for administration at Casino del Sol, the Yaqui tribal enterprise. "People who see me in the casino now, they'll stop and say, 'Hey, how did you get in there?'"

About Martín she says, "I stuck with it for a long time. Too long." But there were "times we were doing really well." As well as some strange accommodations.

"The kids and I had a tradition. For a long time, for one weekend out of the month Martín would take off and go on a drinking binge from Friday until Sunday. He'd come home Sunday and sleep all day. During that time we would go, buy Wienerschnitzel, come home, lie down and watch a movie, and go to sleep. And they liked it. They knew once Martín was gone, 'Can we go buy Wienerschnitzel now?'

"He knew he could go do whatever and come back. He had that control. Either we deal with him or we lose him. I would have my daughter begging, 'Please let my daddy stay.'"

Marisa constantly punctuates her speech with a second language—laughter. It's an expressive and subtle counterpoint. There's sheer pleasure, the full, pealing laugh. There's the conspiratorial giggle. Her laugh can be sober, rueful, or abrupt and sad. Mystified. At times even a touch bitter. At this range it could be called a reflex against pain, but I find more than that in it—a defiance against adversity. Life is supposed to be good, the laugh seems to say. What I'm telling you is just an aberration.

"Martín is a really, really good person," she insists. "The choices he's made are not the choices for our family, I guess." The history of gang violence, chronic addictions, imprisonment, and domestic chaos amounts to "negative choices" and "wrong decisions."

"Everybody," she says, "once they got to know him as a person, they really like him. To this day my family—when it comes to my relationship with him they know I'm doing what's best for me, but at the same time they really care about him as a person. They still hope he's fine. He can stop by my family's house, and they'll welcome him. I think that's why it was so hard to let go for a long time.

"My mom got to accept him, too. When Martín and I were fighting, she would go on his side!" Laughter. "She knew a person like that needed help."

But soon after I'd interviewed Martín, "he was out there making his choices. Once he gets out of his focus, he's gone. The last three months, it was like not knowing who was going to walk in the door. There was no trust. There was nothing."

Even worse, "I started seeing I was changing. I was starting to be a mean person. I was feeding into the arguing, the fighting just like he was. Iliana is vocal about how she feels. She let me know. This isn't who I am. I'm not a miserable person. I'm not a mean person. I realized I needed to get away from him."

Meanwhile, at Casino del Sol Marisa has advanced from answering phones to troubleshooting—beverage machines to computers—for the entire complex, two casinos and a performance stage. An IT Technician, she's awaiting promotion to Specialist.

"They told me, 'You started picking up on so much, just by listening.' They started teaching me little things, then more and more. Now I can actually build a computer. Yeah, it's pretty neat.

"They always tell me, 'You're going to be manager.' It's funny. For my interview with the manager, he asked me, 'Where do you want to be five years from now?'

"I said, 'I want your job.' But it was a joke.

"He said, 'O.K, we'll make it happen.'

"Right now I'm not comfortable having people under me, telling them what to do. I'm not ready. Not yet. But management tells me all the time, 'You have the potential to lead.'

"I'm thirty!" Marisa exclaims. "It's funny because I didn't know. I still feel like I'm twenty-eight. A friend—he's the same age as Martín—was saying, 'You're going to be thirty,' and I was like, 'No, I'm not. I'm twenty-eight.' He said, 'No, you're twenty-nine. Martín is going to be twenty-eight.' I said, 'What?' How did I lose that time? So much stuff was going on I didn't even think about it."

I haven't seen Marisa in almost twenty years, when she
would babysit my toddler daughter during ArtsReach events
at Richey. Now I produce an unpublished piece of her writing
from fifth grade. I'd assigned the class an imaginary biography of
myself. About my old age and death Marisa contributed:

> He was 100,000 years old. He was very ill because
> he was a wino. His parents were 100,000,000
> years old, but they didn't care about him because
> he was a wino. He died standing up. They gave
> him a fancy funeral. The coffin was made of Nice
> 'N' Soft toilet paper. His hair was a toupee. His
> roses were made of moldy, smelly rags. That's why
> it was so fancy.

This is the big laugh.

The new household seems to be forging on. Marisa's
mother, Marta Yucupicio, adds income with two part-time jobs
and "helps me deal with what I have to. I think it helps her, too, to
have us here with her, to not focus on what she went through.
    "I like this little house," Marisa says. "Hopefully, later,
option to buy. You never know."
    The children have had different experiences of their father,
and are adjusting in their own ways.
    "Iliana's seen a lot," Marisa says. "She remembers Martín's
absences, alcohol abuse, substance abuse. She's seen him do
things, be around certain people. And she asks questions. She's not
afraid." In fourth grade, Iliana wrote a mordantly entertaining tale
for me, "The Promise," more reminiscent of her father than her
mother.
    "Iliana has her dad's temper and his personality,
sometimes," Marisa agrees, "but at the same time she has my
strength."
    Most recently, Iliana won recognition for a comic book,

"Graffiti Girl," completed with another ArtsReach instructor, Marge Pellegrino. The heroine combats gangster tagging…with which her father once defaced the Old Pascua neighborhood.

Martín, Jr., has grown up largely without a father, who, as a fugitive and then inmate of the county jail and state prison, missed all his son's birthdays until the fifth.

As a first grader, Martín, Jr., had seemed to hide behind a curtain of long, straight hair, writing little even for his age.

Once again Martín, Sr., is on the run, in hiding; shortly after Marisa left him, he was implicated in another drive-by.

For moments Marisa will speak of him as fondly as if they were a thriving couple.

"Our first date was a big AIDS benefit. He was in sixth, I was in eighth," she reminisces. "I was best friends with his cousin Stephanie. He kind of tried to get to me through her, and finally, I guess, he did." Huge laugh. "He was persistent enough.

"If you asked me three months ago, did I think I was going to be here today without him, I didn't even think about it. I got dependent on the idea of having somebody.

"Thinking back, I couldn't be who he was. I couldn't be irresponsible, I guess. I didn't have time for that. I've never been too irresponsible. Besides my relationship with him." Another laugh. "But I don't have any regret. I can't cry about it or think about it now. If I hadn't been through it, I wouldn't be the person I am today."

While Martín was in prison, Marisa recalls, "he was what they call the pipe holder. He was leading the sweat lodges. Being that person, he had to be pure. He couldn't do anything wrong. Once he got home, into that same lifestyle, he just forgot all about the purity. When I talked to him last, he told me himself, 'Sometimes I just feel like going back [to prison]. I felt good then.'"

Five months later, in November, we're sitting on the same couch, in the same snug house. But Marisa's mother has moved out, and Marisa and her children soon will quit their home, too.

During the entire interview Marisa tensely hugs a cushion to her chest, except when Martín, Jr., burrows his face between her shoulder and the couch arm, or lies on her lap while she strokes his hair.

"Where do I start?" Marisa says.

There were portents.

Even two years before, after Martín was released from prison, "a few incidents really made me scared of him," Marisa says now. "The whole reason my mother was staying here was because of that."

Once Martín broke the windows in Marisa's house and car. Marisa called the police, but when they arrived he had gone.

"Yeah, he'd hit me before," she says now. After "an incident" in the village of Guadalupe, Martín was arrested and fined for disorderly conduct. Marisa's request for a restraining order was denied because of insufficient prior police reports.

After Marisa left Martín this final time, he quickly skidded downhill. Already a fugitive because of the alleged drive-by, he called Marisa one morning at 4 to tell her he'd been shot. A month later, the wound still untreated, she drove him to a clinic. "I'd happened to see him out on the street. The wound was oozing. It looked infected."

His appearance shocked her. "He wasn't even showering. He was nasty. The last few months that I saw him, he didn't even care. Iliana saw him in this Hawaiian print shirt. She said, 'What is my dad wearing?' We said, 'That's not him.'

"He said, 'I can't let go anymore.' He was using a new drug. He was too far into it. It really had him." She would learn it was heroin.

One afternoon, Marisa returned home with Iliana and her godsister to find a skunk in the yard. "It was letting us know that something evil was around," Marisa says. "I believe stuff like that."

Marisa dreamed that a snake was following her. "I said, 'Oh, it's Martín.'" Marisa giggles.

A woman friend told her, "When you dream about a

snake, somebody is trying to do something to you." The friend's son dreamed that Martín was driving Marisa in a car, that he deliberately crashed into a wall, and she died. "The dream felt so bad, and it seemed so real, that he woke up scared." He made his mother call Marisa's home, where Mrs. Yucupicio assured them that Marisa was sleeping peacefully in the next room.

Martín began phoning, jealous. While Iliana visited her godfather one weekend, Marisa explains, "I'd finally let my son spend the night with Martín's mom, because Martín was staying away from there. But it got turned around and twisted. 'Marisa was all alone.' It got him thinking, where was I?

"He kept asking me. I said, 'None of your business.' He called again. 'Are you ready to tell me where you were?' I said, 'Stop calling me.' So I kind of knew something was coming up."

On the night of October 3, about 11:30, Martín began knocking on the windows. "I didn't want the kids to wake up, they were asleep for school. He got me to open the door. He asked me for ice because something was wrong with his hand. He actually came in to tell me he had gotten into some kind of altercation. He was rambling, he was drunk.

"We went in the kitchen. He asked if he could have pizza, and I said, 'Go ahead.' He started warming it up. All of a sudden, 'Give me a hug.'

"I said, 'No, I don't want to hug you.'

"So he got mad. I must have someone else if I didn't want to hug him. Going back to where was I on the weekend.

"It was a revolver, a .38. He opened it up right here by the door. At one point he told me he was taking out the bullets, but I didn't see if he really took them out or not."

By then the children were awake, watching. "He threatened to kill me in front of my kids. I didn't want for the gun to go off. It was scary to think that my kids were here. I just kept telling them to go to their rooms. My daughter wouldn't go. She said, 'No. If I leave, he's going to kill you.' She was thinking if she was present he wouldn't do anything.

"He kept putting the gun to my head, and he shot it. He pulled the trigger. That's what scared my daughter. She would yell. He said there was one bullet in there, that it was a five-round gun. So he would put it at my head and shoot it, and say that I was lucky that it didn't go off. Four times. Pulled the trigger, talked some more stuff, pulled the trigger again. It was awful to think that…I get mad, I get sad, I think, How could he do that? How could he think he could take my life?

"For a half hour or 45 minutes he had me pinned to the couch. I couldn't move. If I got up, he physically pushed me down.

"All of a sudden he just passed out. Leaning on my arm, so I couldn't move. I didn't want to move him and wake him up." Marisa laughs. "It was awful. My daughter got up, got the gun, and put it away to hide it from him. I don't think we would have gotten away if she hadn't done what she did. I asked her to call the cops, but she said, 'I don't know what to say.'

"Iliana got her brother. Since they'd been asleep, she had to get their shoes together. She got my purse, my car keys, everything, being really, really quiet. She got in the car and started the car for me. I told her, 'I'm just going to run out.' We're whispering to each other. I'm talking in her ear. 'I'll give you time. Just go get in the car. I'll be right there. I'm just trying to try to get away from him.' I waited until she got in the car. They went out the back door. I got away. We called the police and they came."

Even then the ordeal wasn't over. After leaving her house around 2 in the morning, the police returned four hours later. Someone had been shot at the drug house Martín frequented. The officer warned Marisa, "I'm not comfortable with you being here at home, knowing that Martín's friends are out there with guns. I would leave."

For a day, she and the kids did. "Martín had so much power that he could ask one of his friends to do something, and they probably would listen."

Almost paradoxically, Marisa is reminded of a clearer, soberer Martín. "When we were living in the apartment, a guy got stabbed." Though enemies, both men involved called Martín. Marisa laughs. "One said, 'Hey, I need your help if these guys come back.' Five minutes later the other guy calls. 'Hey...' Martín hung up and said, 'I'm not going over there.'"

For years, worse phone calls than this would leak from Martín's dark world into their home. Yet except when he'd assaulted her personally, Marisa could divorce herself from his violent nature.

"When it came to him doing all that stuff, I was never around. Just because he knew that wasn't me, that wasn't my life. I didn't talk to him much about it. I didn't care to know. His friends knew that if he was with me, they left him alone. Unless stuff got really bad, I guess."

Now that the reality has so brutally invaded her, Marisa sounds as wistful as she is angry.

"He had one focus when he was on drugs, and that was to be a bad-ass. He lived up to it. It's funny that he could be loyal to that and to his friends, and he just couldn't be loyal to our relationship and to our love. Because I could. When it came to loyalty to his friends and the gang, they had him. And drugs and stuff. I guess they were more exciting than me." She laughs a little.

In the aftermath, the household is still shaken. Martín, Jr., told his teacher, "The other night my daddy came to the house and tried to kill my mom." The children are undergoing counseling. "I didn't think my son was so affected by it, but I guess he's that type of quiet person. He won't talk to me about it. My daughter will talk to me about it. Every day we deal with it," Marisa says.

"My daughter's really hurt because she was a daddy's girl. She always defended him. Now she says, 'I don't want to hear anything about him.' She's cut all ties with him."

Marisa's mother, Marta, had moved out before Martín's attack. "I guess she thought I was defending him too much," Marisa believes. "She's very opinionated.

"The kids want to leave. They've wanted to leave since that night."

Marisa and her children will be packing up to move again, this time to Alberto Yucupicio's, her father's, house. He has just begun dialysis. "He says, 'Just move in with me so I can take care of you guys, and you can take care of me.'"

I ask, does she consider leaving Old Pascua behind altogether?

Marisa laughs indulgently at me. "It's like you said once, you're on the outside looking in." Old Pascua is her comfort, she explains. "People in the neighborhood look out for each other. I had people coming over. 'If you ever need anything, just call me.' My neighbor is keeping a close eye, sometimes even reporting to my mom. They'll see someone and they'll come and knock. 'Are you O.K.?'"

The personal trauma hasn't slowed Marisa's professional ascent at Casino del Sol, where she's made the jump from IT Technician to IT Specialist. In an industry founded upon gambling, she's involved with what may be the biggest gamble of all, as the casino switches its entire gaming program from Oasis to the rival IGT. "I'm scared about the technology because it's so new," Marisa admits.

"Scared" may be a relative word, after what she's endured. As much as anything, she seems eager and excited. Less reluctant to lead, she has gained confidence in her own management style. "I'm not demanding. If you want a certain reaction, if you want a result, you've got to do it the right way. I've just been me. Even my directors say, 'If you ask the guys to do something, you know they'll do it.'

"I have a feeling of my own potential," Marisa says. "Any person has the potential to do anything if they only go and do it."

She struggles to see the potential in Martín, serving a ten-year prison term for the assault.

"I will always care for him. That's the sad part. That's what hurts. You know a person, how good they can be, and to see them that way…I still pray for him. I'm human. I have a heart. I'm a forgiving person. I don't pass judgment. I'm sure if Martín were to call me out of the blue and apologize, I would probably accept it.

"It doesn't mean that I would accept him back into my life," she adds quickly. "I can't live with hurt and anger in my heart. I just can't. Just like I can't fall asleep at night mad. That's awful to go to sleep that way.

"I'll never trust him again. I'm not going to put anything past him anymore. I know all sides of Martín. I know him better than he knows himself. That's where he became dependent on me. If I could breathe for him, he would let me. It was like I was living him.

"He's an adult. He needs to do it on his own. Tough love.

"I've got to see the positive in it. He's in jail. He's safer, and people are safe from him. It's really sad what happened, but if I had to go through that, hurting that pain, for him to get better, then I'm willing to do it. If Martín had to do that to get through what he needed to, then I was happy to help, in a strange way."

# The Promise

One day at school there was a little girl had a problem because everybody would make fun of her. I didn't know why, but I would ask people why are they laughing at her? But they just laughed and laughed. So I went to that girl. I asked her, "Why are all those people laughing at you?"

She said, "Do you really want to know?"

I said, "Yes."

She said, "I'll show you, but only if you promise not to get scared or tell anyone."

So I said, "I promise."

So she showed me, and she had a lot of scars. Not to be mean, but they were ugly. And do you know what happened? I broke my promise and got scared and screamed all the way home.

*—Iliana Acuña, 4th Grade*

—*Angela Francisco*

# EUCARIO MENDEZ

Eucario "Chapo" Mendez is of mixed descent, his father a member of the Zapotec and other tribes from the Oaxaca region of Mexico, his mother Mexican-American, born in Mexico City.

He grew up in the largely Yaqui neighborhood of Old Pascua, where he still lives.

"Until I was, oh, in elementary sometime, I thought I was Yaqui!" he says.

# Mr. John

His name is J.R. He wears black pants and a head band. And he likes to make rhymes when he wants to.

His face is oval and his ears are small. He walks like a cool dude. His goal is to get a job at Target.

One morning J.R. got up for his interview, so he took a shower and was thinking about what he will say. "Hi, good morning, Mr. John, what's going on, Na, Na."

He got out and put on his black Levi pants and his head band to impress Mr. John. J.R. was walking down the street when he saw the store, Target. He got in, and when he opened the door to the office he saw a great big table looking to the other side. There he was, fat, wearing guest clothes with a tie and good-looking pants. He was eating a great big chocolate bar.

J.R. was nervous and he said, "Hi, Mr. John, I'm glad to meet you, Ya, Ya, Ya."

"Thank you," Mr. John said in a grumpy voice. Mr. John then said a lot of questions. And J. R. kept on saying, "Yes, yes, yes."

Then Mr. John was scratching his head, and while he was scratching his toupee fell. Mr. John put it on fast. Then he said, "No. You can't have the job."

"But why?" J.R. said.

"Look at your clothes, you got to be like me."

"I will change."

"First change, then come for a job."

"OK."

The next day J.R. got all of his money he had saved and bought guest clothes like Mr. John, but skinnier, of course. His suit was gray with good-looking black pants and a red tie.

Now he had to change his attitude.

The next day J.R. was thinking how he would change. Then it hit him. He found an idea. He was to spy on Mr. John for at least 3 days because he wanted to get that job as soon as possible. So he got his black Levis and his head band and went to Mr. John's house.

When he got to Mr. John's house, J.R. got on the window and heard a loud screaming voice that made J.R. fall from the window. Then he got up and saw Mr. John screaming at his wife. For the last three days Mr. John screamed at his wife.

Now J.R. was practicing to yell like Mr. John did.

"Hi, do you remember me? I'm the guy who didn't look so neat." After he practiced for two days he went to Mr. John's office.

When it was morning, he got up and took a shower and got his guest clothes and went to the store. When he opened the door, there Mr. John was again, big and fat and eating a chocolate bar.

Then J.R. said in a yelling voice, "Hi, do you remember me? I'm the guy who didn't look so neat."

Then Mr. John jumped up and he said, "Yes, that's what I want. You can be an assistant manager. But how did you change?"

"By spying on you."

"Spying on me?" Mr. John said.

"Yes, and I can yell just like you yell at your wife at home."

Then Mr. John was shy, nervous, and was so angry that he was as hot as a tea kettle, because J.R. found out about his secret. Then Mr. John said, "You're fired."

—*Eucario Mendez, 6th Grade*

# The Desert

As I walk in the desert
I see a coral snake passing by,
and the bright sun shines the day.

I hear birds singing on a
mesquite tree. I hear animals
crying for food and water.

I feel a strong breeze passing by,
and the animals come to me
so I can touch them.

So, the next time you are in
a desert, like me, see things,
feel things, and hear things.

*—Eucario Mendez, 6$^{th}$ Grade*

◎  ◎  ◎  ◎  ◎  ◎

"Mr. John" could be read as a sly thrust at the hypocrisy of the dominant class, its cultural arrogance in forcing conformity. So I've presented it to decades of elementary school students and their teachers. J.R.'s transformation from the happy-go-lucky barrio kid to the screaming apprentice of Mr. John is told with expert pacing, humor, and economy of detail. The barrio headband itself seems to morph into the corporate tie, as one reader has pointed out. Ultimately, J.R. is undone by the innocence and honesty that shame his prospective boss.

Except the author doubts he meant it that way.

"Maybe I didn't have that insight," says Eucario "Chapo" Mendez. "I was in my own little world back then, entertaining myself, I guess."

I remember that, too, the winter of 1987, Chapo scribbling furiously at the back of the classroom, pausing every now and then to chuckle at his own words. Short—"Chapo" means "Shorty"—vibrant, with glossy hair and skin, he resembled the J.R. of his creation.

No anger at the Mr. Johns of the world, the social injustice they could represent?

"I go with the flow. I'm easygoing."

What does "Mr. John" mean to Chapo?

"J.R. might have been like me when I was young. My dad always said you work for what you want, and you can get it. Preaching that to us. Work, work. Maybe that's how the story came across, trying to get a job. I was 11 years old."

So that's it. "Mr. John" isn't subversive, political satire. It's about looking for a job.

Now thirty-one and a sturdy five foot, eight inches tall, Chapo has an even keener incentive to stay employed. "The most important thing in my life right now is family. Supporting my kids." These are his son, also Eucario, and stepson, Francisco Villa, both elementary school students. We're talking in the living room of his parents' house in the primarily Yaqui barrio of Old Pascua, where he lives with the boys, his parents, and his girlfriend, Tricia. It is the fall of 2006.

Though Chapo and Francisco's mother split long ago, Chapo has raised the boy as his own since he was one. "He went through some rough times," Chapo says, without elaborating. "He's real quiet. He's into himself. He likes to be alone."

"My son is Eucario Javier Mendez. I'm Eucario Cornelio Mendez. I wanted him to have a pronounceable middle name." Chapo laughs. Like his dad, Eucario Javier is "real outgoing."

Clearly, Chapo thrives on activity of all kinds. When I first spoke with him, his weekly schedule included soccer, volleyball, billiards, and a neighborhood baseball tournament. He's just as involved with his sons. Along with helping them do their homework, he coaches their community soccer team. On weekends he helps organize games for them and other neighborhood kids.

The family commitment is another tradition. "Our family, we did get disciplined," Chapo remembers. "We did have structure. Just sitting down with your family eating dinner, even once a week. We still have our cookouts. My father will go outside and cook *carne asada*, steaks. Call everybody to come."

An old-fashioned word begins attaching itself to Chapo: virtuous. Work hard. Do right by others. And don't grouse about it. Maybe that's why a sociological interpretation of "Mr. John" leaves him cold. The Mr. Johns are a fact of existence. Deal with it. Move on.

Chapo took his first job at age fourteen. "You see those guys walking around selling candy or ice cream pops with the little bell? I used to do that." He worked a concession stand at the University of Arizona's basketball court "so I could watch all the games." He sold bagels at the university and clothing at Factory

2-U. He even tried telemarketing—"you change your voice, this nice person, really trustworthy, to get them to buy this credit card or whatever. I was always working. I wanted to keep busy. I wanted to have money, to hang out."

When he was eighteen, Chapo's work ethic took on a larger dimension, after he was shot in the leg. "We were at a concert, not a gang concert or anything. It was a Mexican concert. We were out there being teenagers, trying to pick up women, you know. Cars were talking to other cars. I was getting out of our car. This guy just goes—you want to get shot? Boom. There it was. I was just in the way.

"That was a life-changing experience. That's probably what made me want to work with children, get them away from that life into a different life, something better."

For over a decade, Chapo devoted himself to programs for troubled youth—Arizona Children's Association, Vision Quest, HomeQuest, finally the Catalina Mountain School under the Department of Juvenile Corrections. At various times he served as teacher's aide, group home leader, counselor, and guard.

Many memories are fond. "I wouldn't have done it so long if I didn't enjoy what I was doing." At the HomeQuest alternative school he learned the therapeutic power of animals. "Some of these kids' backgrounds are really horrible. They have a lot of anger problems. They're real emotional and real fragile, and anything could trigger them. What helped was feeding the horses. That was one thing they wanted to do. They'd come up and ask you. It would take a while to load up the bales, drive, feed the horses. That's when you can use the one-on-one, talking to the kids, what's on your mind? Anything going on at home?

"The whole cliché, if you affect one person's life…I see some of these kids, they were ten years old, now they're nineteen and they have their jobs, and their families. They say they're doing good, they're staying away from that other stuff, and that brings a good sigh of relief."

The more harrowing experiences, Chapo tells with

characteristic equanimity. "I've been assaulted. I never felt scared. To my mind, come on, they're kids. Maybe some of them are big, six foot five, muscular, they can be athletes, star football players. I never felt endangered. I never got in a situation one-on-one. I could sit there with twenty kids, no problem. If something went down, I just call for backup. You have your radio.

"Nothing really surprised me," Chapo maintains. "Well, actually, there was one. A youth tried to hang himself. I happened to be in his area. I looked in the window, about eight by eight, I saw his feet first, and I looked up. I popped open his door and just grabbed him. He was already tying the knot around his neck. I picked up his legs—he was on one of those bunk beds. He was about to step off. He was fourteen, fifteen years old. When I stopped him, he didn't change his demeanor. I believe he didn't even say anything. Afterward he went to another institution. He had chewed some glasses also, a light bulb, he broke it, tried to eat it. There were a lot of issues going on with him."

Almost exactly a year before our interviews, Chapo abruptly quit the Catalina Mountain School, giving his two weeks' notice. He blames the rigors and stress of the job less than the bureaucracy. "You start doing a program, then the authorities come down, we're changing that, we've got to do it this way now. It wasn't consistent. It seemed the laws changed every month. It's confusing to us, and it's confusing to the juveniles even more. It takes a lot out of you." Increasingly, as co-workers begged off, Chapo was called upon to do double shifts. "It was taking me away from my own kids. When I came home I was too tired to do anything with them. I thought, I don't belong here any more." As if catching himself in complaint, he adds, "It was a good experience, though."

Tempted to use the time off to earn his degree, abandoned long before after two years at a community college, instead Chapo found himself back on the job almost immediately. "My friend said, 'Come work at the swimming pool company, it's easy.'

At first the suggestion rankled Chapo's professional pride.

"I didn't want to be a pool guy. That's not a respectable job, or something. This job is a break. It's not something for a career."

But, perhaps to his own puzzlement, Chapo has found pool maintenance a welcome antidote to his years of social work. "It's relaxing being by myself. I have my own truck. A lot of driving. A lot of thinking. Listen to the radio. Some of the swimming pools are pretty messed up, but I go to nice pools, too, look around the layout, the houses overlooking the city. Think about what they do for a living, because it's a nice house. Doctors, lawyers. It's real peaceful. It's calm. I get houses where people are from back east, you know. They buy houses and come down here just for the winter. They have this house just for when they want it—they have their maids that come and water the plants, dust it all off. I wonder what they're doing now, in New York, or traveling. I'd be over here at this house! Just sit here and have some cold ones. What more do you want?"

It's all too tempting to draw conclusions about the shape of another's entire life, based on brief acquaintance, a few conversations, a story and poem. But Chapo's job history does align so neatly with his old writings. "Mr. John" is all action, striving, disappointment, as if foretelling the intensity and grind of his ten-year career in the trenches. Meanwhile, the sixth-grade poet replenished himself in nature, advising his readers to contemplate, to "see things, feel things, and hear things," just as Chapo does now.

Chapo describes: "One pool up by Sabino Canyon, when it rained, the water was flowing through the creek, you could hear it hitting the rocks. I just stood there watching, how much water comes down those mountains, it's unbelievable. Did it rain this much? It's nice and cool up there, before I come back to town. See a couple of frogs. I came across a desert tortoise. You come across tarantulas, scorpions. They don't bother me. I just watch them go. Lizards I saved from the pool. Snakes—I'd rather see them out there than at home. I saw a dark black snake dart across, rabbits, coyotes, all kinds of wildlife. I've seen a javelina. We live so close to the desert, which is cool.

"I'm moving up in positions at the pool company. I'm training a couple of new people. My supervisor was asking if I could help out, and I said sure. And the pay is awesome! More than I was getting paid doing my other job. I used to come home cranky. Now I don't come back all mad."

Chapo seems to lead a good, balanced life, I tell him.

"I try. I don't need to be great at anything. I just want to try. I'm satisfied where I'm at. I'm happy. I'm not on the streets or anything. I have no regrets for anything that happened. I have no regrets for anything I've done. It's all part of growing up."

Absorbed in work and family, the adult Eucario Mendez has given little thought to writing. "I could have pursued it more. I liked writing when I was younger. As I got older, you don't have time for it."

He remembers receiving the ArtsReach booklet, but "back then, you don't realize how valuable it is later on in life. I probably used it to put under the leg of a table or something." Still, being published impressed him. "Especially growing up, it was hard here, my parents speaking Spanish, and I just couldn't believe it." Then his poem, "The Desert," was selected for the Arlene Hirschfelder-Beverly Singer anthology *Rising Voices: Writings of Young Native Americans.* "I said yeah! Because they said, 'we're going to pay you money.' A lot. Right away I decided, here you go. Do whatever you want with it. Sign my rights away. And they sent me the book also."

Eventually he lost both books, "moving from here to there."

Now he marvels at "Mr. John" as if it were written by someone else. "Just reading this story, I go, Wow, man! Even when I went to Pima College, this is way better than what I wrote there, or what I wrote in high school. It's so well put. It just blows me away." He even wonders if I might have doctored it before publication, but I assure him the words are his, that I probably could dig up a copy of the written draft to show him, since I hoard student work. My shed is bursting with boxes of yellowing, crumbling looseleaf from twenty years ago, that I can't bear to throw away.

Though somewhat intimidated by his own sixth-grade achievement, Chapo is game to try a new piece of writing. For this second session, I'm sitting on a tool chest in his back yard. "My dad," he explains, gesturing at the junked cars surrounding us. "He gets off work and look—he just has to keep busy. Work, work. That's where I get it from."

During our interviews, no question of mine, or response or memory of his own, had seemed to ruffle Chapo's good nature. Despite a glancing reference here and there to anger, he never displayed a flicker of it. Being shot was "a big mix-up." About the stress of managing troubled kids while being squeezed in the bureaucratic vise, he concluded mildly, "I think I might have just got burned out. I might go back later on. I just need to re-energize." (He reserved his outrage for country music: "I hate it. Go to Circle K's, country everywhere. I want to get my stuff and leave, but there's a line—aah, torturing me!")

It was almost stunning, then, to read the voice that emerged from his brief writings in the back yard, comfortably strewn with his father's projects. Bitterly humorous, the Corrections pieces also display the confident pacing and shaping of a storyteller conscious of audience. As a writer, the laid-back Chapo pounces on his material.

Our writing self and our daily self may be twins, but they are scarcely identical.

The pool cleaner episode yields a final insight: here is a job one actually can complete. A pool is dirty, you clean it, mission accomplished. Not like the perpetually unfinished task of trying to fix human lives.

# Work Sketches

### *Officer Mendez*

Pulling up to the job site, I see the high fences with razor-sharp barb wires. The coldness of the wind coming down the mountains as if to say, "Stay away." I walk through the metal detectors which don't even work. The security officer moves the metal detector like a magic wand all around your body. No beeping, of course, because it doesn't work. As I walk up the hill I feel as if I am a "dead man walking." As I look all around me I see my co-workers walking like zombies, slower and slower they walk, not wanting to enter.

As I enter the building and say goodbye to the night watchman, I don't even get done saying "bye." The night watchman storms out of the building. The smell of old clothes that haven't been dried in days is in the air. Six a.m., walking down the hallway, inserting the keys, one door open, two doors open, now all doors open. One by one as doors unlock I say, "Time to get up, clean your room."

The response at first is silence. Then seconds later, "Close my fuckin' door," "Fuck you," and finally, "I'm turning eighteen pretty soon. I don't have to do shit." Then I turn around to dock the points for staff disrespect. A voice far down the hall says, "Hey, Mendez, can I get the mop and broom to clean my room?" I say "yes" and come back to reality, and do my job as best as I can.

Beep Beep the alarm sounds. Five-thirty in the morning, don't want to wake up. Don't want to hear the officers at the gate gossiping about what happened the night before, and how our unit is not being run correctly.

Well, now out of the shower, time to pick up

the phone. I cough to say these words, "This is Officer Mendez out of Agave. I have a bad cold and I'll not be coming in today." Click.

## The Pool

Arriving at the shop to pick up my supplies and route sheet, I look to see where my day will be spent. Ah, I'm going to the foothills. As I leave the shop I tell everyone to have a good day. Driving toward my destination, I see the sun rising slowly above the Catalina Mountains. My window is rolled down to feel the good clean air. As I get closer and closer, I leave the city and enter a different world, away from all the smog, traffic, and road rage. Pull up to my first house. I slowly get out of my truck still amazed by the sunrise and birds all around, playing. I grab my pole and supplies to clean the pool. It's good to be alone with no one to bug me.

The water is clear as glass. I look at the bottom before I disturb the peacefulness of the water. As I put my net in, the ripples flow outwards and end when they hit the tile. I put the net down to the deep end to pick up a poor rabbit that must have gotten spooked and hopped its way into the pool. I continue netting all the bird feathers that fell into the pool as if they just got done bathing. I'll net the pool until it's clean, then I switch the net to a brush. I brush the entire pool to collect the dirt that collected on the sides. I take my chemicals from the box and check to make sure there's chlorine, and they're well balanced. I make one last look at the pool to make sure it is clean enough where I would want to swim in it. Yes, it is time to move on.

*Eucario Mendez, 2006*

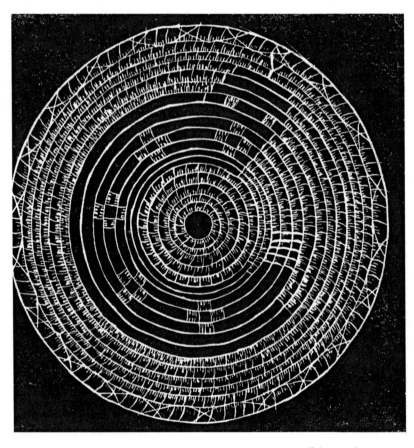

*—Dionne Lopez*

# JOSEPHINE FRYE

Josephine "Josie" Frye is a member of the Tohono O'odham tribe. Born in Eloy, Arizona, she now lives in Covered Wells, on the Tohono O'odham Nation.

# A Story About My Grandmother

It's 1941, May 4. On a cloudy day, a little girl named Lucy is throwing rocks in a little pond nearby where she lives. She lives in a village called Friendly Corner. Then her mother comes out and starts to talk about what the rocks feel when they're moved and thrown.

After her mother is finished talking about the rocks, she looks at the sky and begins to cry. Her daughter looks at her and asks her what's wrong. Her mother doesn't answer, but she grabs Lucy and takes her inside. Lucy looks at the time. It is almost time for her father to come home. He works out on a field. Soon Lucy looks outside the window and sees her mother getting the clothes off the clothesline. Lucy notices that the clothes are flying up, and her mother's hair is getting blown into her face.

When she comes inside, she gets Lucy and they both sit in a corner of the house. Lucy asks, "What's going on?" Her mother hugs her and says that "A big windstorm is coming, and I don't know where your father is."

"But how do you know there is a windstorm coming?"

Her mother asks Lucy if she remembers when she told her that her mother's legs would hurt when it was going to rain, and if her hands would hurt it was going to rain with thunder and lightning. And Lucy says, "Yes, I remember." Then they are quiet for a while. Her mother says that she is feeling the same things, only she cries when it's windy. She guesses the reason is because it's the opposite of wet. When the wind hits you when you're wet, you get dry.

After it gets really windy, the door flies open and in walks Lucy's father. He goes over to them and sits by them, and they all hug each other and wait until the wind calms down. But about twenty minutes later a tornado is coming. It hits, but misses their house. Then a big rock comes through the window, and the rock has a drawing on it. The drawing is a feather. Lucy saw the rock somewhere before. They just sit still until the tornado goes away. When it finally does go away, Lucy remembers what her mother said about the rocks, so Lucy picks the rock up and puts it back where she saw it. It is back with its family, and so is Lucy.

—*Josie Frye, 7th Grade*

# This Woman

I stood seeing this woman I
    thought I knew.
Her hair, reddish black
    like blood from a deep wound.
Her eyes black-brown like wood
    from the mesquite tree.
Her complexion a light brown, like
    the sands of the hot, dry desert.
Her lips full, almost perfect like the
    quarter moon when she would smile.
I stood hearing her voice
    so beautiful and as silent
    as the whisper of the wind.
I stood smelling the sweetness of
    her perfume, like a flower
    in bloom.
To me this woman was beautiful.
I stood looking at my reflection in
    the mirror.

—*Josie Frye, 10th Grade*

# Rain

Standing outside.
I see the clouds rushing my way.
The shadow of my house grows long, as the sun
    hides behind the west mountains.
The mountains to the east, which is where
    Baboquivari and Kitt Peak stand together, outlined
    by the dark purple sky.
I hear the wind as it starts to whisper, loud,
    louder.
The rumble of thunder like the beating on the
    sacred drum.
It grows darker, the shadow of my house
    disappears.
Then it begins to rain, the drops pound against
    the desert floor like feet of the sacred dancers.
I smell the wet dirt, so good. It makes me
    want to take a chunk of the dirt to taste
    like when I was first born.
Standing outside. The rain has passed.

*—Josie Frye, 11th Grade*

# Is It "I Am" Or "My Name"

My name belongs to a dead white woman. How it got
   down to me?
I don't know. Josephine. Does not suit me. It has no
   meaning
But I am a meaning, a meaning for laughter
Like a feather of the eagle being patted over a child's
   body for blessing.
   The child laughs.
I am a meaning, a meaning for strength
Like a feather of the eagle being patted over my
   grandfather's body
   for blessing. My grandfather who is a warrior.
I am a meaning, a meaning of gentleness
Like a feather of the eagle being patted over my mother's
   body
   for blessing. My mother a heroine.
I am a meaning, a meaning of a birthmark.
Like a feather of the eagle being patted over my body for
   blessing. My name Spotted Feather.
   Not just my name it's who I am.

*—Josie Frye, 11ᵗʰ Grade*

# Listen

As the wind blows and whistles in the night, she speaks
As the smell of the greasewood trees gets stronger, they
    speak
As the clouds rumble over the lands of the desert, she
    speaks
As the moon shines down on the earth, they make love
As erosion occurs and the land has changed, she speaks
As the cactus flower blooms at its usual time, she has
    given birth
As the sun rises and sets through the days, he laughs
As mother earth, father sky, brother sun, and sister wind
    speak, listen.

—*Josie Frye, 11ᵗʰ Grade*

# City's Voice

She ran, breathing hard, beads of
sweat forming on her face.
    The cold winter wind scraping against
her skin as she ran.
    The harder she ran the colder it
got. Still breathing hard.
    As her legs shifted from one in front
of the other, the muscles in her thighs got harder.
    The stinging pain in her calves,
almost cramping.
    Her hair bouncing up every time her legs
took turns stepping on the ground.
    She ran, like a horse, so graceful,
so hard.
    But the hand of the policeman grabbed
the back of her sweatshirt.
    Knocking her to the ground, holding
her down, with her arm twisted behind her.
    As she lay pinned down by the cop, her
left cheek touched the ground.
    She breathed in and out, as the air
blew out her mouth
    the dust on the ground blew up, she
felt the pounding in her chest from her heart.
    So fast, like the revolver heard in the
middle of the night on the streets.
    The cop handcuffed her, read her the
rights she had and sat her in the back of the car.
    Passing the street lights which lit up her
face, every 10 seconds.
    The movement from the car made the shadow
of the cage dance across the back seat.

At the station took fingerprints, thrown
in a cell, sticking her face through the bars,
    holding one in each hand, waiting,
bored out of her mind.
    She ran, made herself a record,
yet she had no voice.

*—Josie Frye, 11ᵗʰ Grade*

# Eclipse and Commode

One time I was bored. There was nothing to do, so
I thought. Anyway, I was about 4, 4 ½ maybe, and I loved
to be in the bathroom. The sound of all the waters in
there was wonderful. I was fascinated by it. To me it was
a place of cleanliness. It was like church, I guess. You
know how they say get your sins washed away. That's
what it was like for me, because I'd be outside playing in
the dirt, making mud thises and thats, and it would be
getting dark, so I'd go in the back door, go straight to the
bathroom, and clean myself up before my mom could yell
at me.

One day, I remember it was about midday or
afternoon, and everyone was so excited, standing outside,
coming in and out of the house. I went outside and saw
people outside their apartments with boxes on their
heads, looking at the sun. Even my mom had one. She
looked ridiculous to me, but I didn't say a thing. (Later
I realized it was the day of the eclipse.) I went back
inside, and from there I went in the bathroom. I was
just in there, flushing the bowl, letting the water run in
the shower and the sink. The sound was so much like a
waterfall out in the wilderness.

I remember what my mother said about keeping
the bathroom clean. In my mind, I could still see her
pouring the Clorox in the bowl and shaking the Ajax in
the sink and tub. So I got the Clorox and poured it in
the bowl, and got the Ajax and sprinkled it all over, in
the sink and the tub and even in the bowl, onto the floor.
It started to bubble like the time my mom was making
popovers. I remembered the bubbles the oil made,
popping onto my mom's arms and burning her. It was the
exact same thing in the bowl, but before it exploded I ran

out to where my mom and the neighbors were.

Soon everyone heard a big "Kaboom!" I ran back inside to the bathroom. It was a mess. A white cloud of smoke filled the room, and you could smell Clorox all over, almost burning your eyes. The commode was split in two and pieces of it were lying everywhere. My mom ran inside and had that look on her face like "I know it was you, you're going to get it!" When I tried to leave, my mom grabbed me and spanked me to high hell.

After that I thought, "Well for sure I ain't gonna be no mad scientist." Here I am a writer.

*—Josie Frye, 11th Grade*

◎ ◎ ◎ ◎ ◎ ◎

Josie Frye was hard to find. For several years I'd tried, phoning her foster mother, Lucilda Norris, asking around. A high school friend, or Josie's foster sister, Amber, would pass on a rumor, a suggestion. Josie was living with a woman in Sacaton, on the Gila River Reservation. No, she was in Gila Bend. Tucson. Covered Wells. My inquiries always arrived one step behind; she had left, to parts unknown. Once I even had a cell phone number, but its reception was limited, and I was out of range. I never reached her.

I wanted to, very much. Of all my talented, beloved students, she was the most a writer. Others wrote with their mind, their heart, their passion, their spirit. Josie's writing draws upon all these, but more, she had the artist's need to grasp the world aesthetically, reinvent it imaginatively. Mark Helprin, in his short story "Tamar," suggests, "Perhaps things are most beautiful… when, for want of connection, the world deepens and becomes art."

Some people buy lottery tickets. I called Josie's foster parents once again, late May, 2008. Her foster father, Marcos Valenzuela, said sure, Josie was a dispatcher for the Tohono O'odham Police, here was the phone number. Within a minute I was speaking to her, arranging to meet the following week.

To the outsider, like me, the reservation can seem like a national park. Ignore the broken bottles along the roads, distressing for their human cost but a superficial scar on the land. The drive to Josie's home, in the Upper Village of Covered Wells, leaves even the rural town of Sells twenty-five miles behind. The road veers and tilts through hills riding into the distance. Mountain ranges in every direction seem to hold the land in place. No ostentatious mansions sprawl upon them. Dirt washes, not

concrete channels, cut the terrain. No parcels are staked out for
multiple homes per acre. It is the desert. It is simply there. On
this particular day saguaro buds are breaking into cream-white
blossoms. Hawks perch on trees and telephone poles, while flocks
of vultures unfurl crooked black wings as if for shade, feeding on
roadkill.

Well, yes, the Border Patrol whooshed by, and those
warplanes did streak across the sky, sharp as darts.

Upper Village is nestled among raw lava hills, a handful of
gray lumps that on closer inspection prove to be mud-adobe brick
wrapped in chicken wire and unpainted stucco.

Inside, the adobe and mud plastering are clearly visible
through gaps in the interior paint. Wooden window sills are dark
and splintered with age. Josie and I sit in easy chairs flanked by
a Bob Marley One Love poster and a painted Asian dancer. Josie
dresses for comfort in sweats and T-shirt. (I remember years ago,
back at her foster parents', she rehearsed for an ArtsReach reading
in her pajamas.) Her face fits the description in her poem, "This
Woman," adding the distinctive birthmark on her cheek. Birds
twitter through the open door, above the whirr of the floor fan,
the home's only cooling.

A worn leatherette binder spreads across Josie's lap, the
writing journal she began some fifteen years before, sheaves of
pages of varying sizes and shades, some browned with age. She has
been revising.

"You know what happened?" she says. "I had a house in
Casa Grande, living by myself, but I was with Lucilda and my dad
for the weekend. I got a call from my neighbors. They told me that
my house burned down. I couldn't believe them until I got there
the next day. It was gone. It was just burnt frame. Everything I had
worked for five years, I lost it all. Everything, the books—thank
God, this didn't burn." She holds up the binder. "It was in the back
room, the only room that didn't burn. I didn't care about anything
else. Just this." Josie's voice trembles. "I cried because I thought I
lost it. I went through the house and found it. It was the happiest

moment in my life.

"It smelled like smoke. It took years for that smell to get out."

Since graduating high school in '97, as best as we can figure, Josie has lived in Tucson, Sacaton, Chandler, Eloy, Casa Grande, Eloy again, Casa Grande again, and Tucson again, before settling in Covered Wells the past two years.

But when I met her, a seventh grader, she already was rootless—uprooted, really. Withdrawn, inward in class, she wrote a hymn to family harmony, "A Story About My Grandmother," while living in a foster home. Her language arts teacher told me Josie was gravely depressed, that she was unlikely to read her story out loud at the University of Arizona, but that it would be healthy for her to be invited, and perhaps even accompany her peers.

Not only did Josie read, but in a thrilling contralto that reminded me of Marian Anderson.

I ask her now, "Do you ever actually sing?"

"I've done karaoke," she laughs. "A lot of people say I'm good."

I remember another reading, to the National Indian Education Association conference, when in the midst of a poem Josie began coughing, then crying. She bowed over the podium while the audience hushed helplessly. I offered her water, to hold the microphone while she composed herself. She refused any assistance. While we waited, she coughed and cried. Without wiping her face, she resumed and finished.

I hadn't presumed to ask about her circumstances, why she had no home. I thought maybe her parents were dead.

Josie's birth mother, Emma, is still very much alive, it turns out, in Eloy, where Josie was born. Josie's last piece of writing, a few months before, was a letter to her. "I wanted to send it, but I just…didn't." Her eyes well up. "My mom chose a man over us when we were growing up. And that was awful."

Josie's wanderings began with that man. [See her poem "His Name," p. 103] At first all lived together, his children and

Emma's—Josie and her older sister, Connie. But the household was constantly, violently disrupted. "I do remember him hitting me. You shouldn't hit kids, you know? He would beat my mom up and I would see that. Then we'd have to leave. We would go to my aunt's house. He would apologize, and we'd go back, and they'd get in a fight again, and we'd go back to my aunt's house. That's how it was when I was little."

Until Josie's fourth or fifth grade. "We weren't his. He didn't want us there, so she sent us to the boarding school." But when Child Welfare learned about the abuse to Josie and especially Connie, "We couldn't go home because of that." The sisters were sent to the Girls' Home in Covered Wells; eventually Josie was moved to the foster home.

While at the Girls' Home, "We took off. I remember like it was yesterday." Josie was about eleven, her sister, thirteen. "I wanted to go see my mom. Connie *said* she wanted to see my other sister. But she wanted to see a guy. She was mad at my mom. She was the first to understand what was really going on."

The girls ended up sleeping in an abandoned van in Eloy, or "in the trees, the bushes. I was so cold. We were right by the side of the road, the cars going by. I got scared.

"I would follow her [Connie] to her guy's house. She would get drunk, and I would watch her.

"I would get hungry, and she would get mad because I was always complaining and crying. I would tell her, 'Let's go back to the Girls' Home. There's beds there, and they're going to feed us.' She said, 'No, I'm not going back there.' We'd go to the supermarket, acting like we're shopping. She'd have a cart, putting the stuff in there. She'd just open the packages and we'd eat in the store. We were never caught. Back then they didn't have the cameras. Then we'd leave the cart and walk out. That's how we'd eat. Then I'd be satisfied and I'd be fine."

But after a week, "I was tired of it. I just wanted to go home. I was crying, 'Let's go back, please.' Connie said, 'You go back if you want to.' I begged her and I cried, 'Please, go back with me.' She said, 'No, I can't take care of you forever.'

"She didn't want to leave. She wanted to be with that guy. That's what I didn't understand. He didn't even give us a place to stay. Why did she want to stay? But she was young, you know. She wanted to get out there and grow up already. He was eighteen or nineteen. She was thirteen, but she looked a lot older. She did the same thing my mom did. She chose a man over me."

By high school, Josie had found an environment that was stable if not entirely comfortable, with foster parents Lucilda Norris and Marcos Valenzuela. She agrees that they are solid people, "but Marcos is the one I'm really, really close to. He looks to me as his daughter." About Lucilda, a judge in tribal courts, Josie says, "It was hard to live up to her standards." Furthermore, "They didn't know I was with another girl. I didn't know how to tell them. I was in the closet, like they say. Lucilda found out on her own. She was kind of pissed about it.

"I left home when I was eighteen. I was gone."

To Tucson. Sacaton. Chandler. And so on. In a poem from her late teens, "Another Society," Josie wrote:

I carry that dust, this dust, his dust,
her dust, and I'm still moving…
picking up dust from people
I don't even know…
I guess I'll just keep walking

In Sacaton, the relationship with a woman "wasn't good. It wasn't home. I just needed to push myself to get out." She tried living in Eloy, with Connie and *her* abusive husband, taking care of Connie's children. Then in Casa Grande, where the house burned. Tucson again, where Josie worked at Desert Diamond Casino, staying in a trailer. Four years ago, she met Lynette Tashquinth at a bar.

The beginnings were not auspicious. The ex-lover from Sacaton, who had followed Josie to Tucson, got in a fistfight with

Lynette. Josie moved in with Lynette, who subsequently was evicted from her rental, along with her brother. All three occupied Josie's trailer, then Lynette's sister-in-law's place. "Everything was horrible then. I felt like nothing was going to get paid and we were going to be homeless." Lynette left; Josie got an apartment; Lynette moved in. "Finally I felt safe because it was just me and her."

Briefly, at least. "It was bad," Josie admits. "Going out too much, drug use, both of us. I felt like, if she's going to do it, then I'm going to do it."

Two years ago, the couple moved to the home in Covered Wells, built by Lynette's great-grandfather, where Lynette had grown up. She could show Josie a dragon she had carved into a lava hillside, as a teenager. "In Tucson it was crowded. The traffic. Here you go outside and actually see the stars."

Josie's and Lynette's decision a year ago to go clean, no drugs or alcohol, may have been a turning point. While Josie works at the police department, Lynette "is just here. She cleans and cooks. It's kind of weird because she does everything I should be doing, because she looks more like a guy, and she's doing the house.

"She makes me happy. She's funny. She sees humor where I don't. She helps me see that. When we're just sitting there, and you see something or hear something—she's artistic, she likes to draw, she sees art in everything, and she helps me see that. It makes life easier.

"I like being here. I wanted to be somewhere that was home."

For most of my subjects in this book, writing is a valued part of their past that must be coaxed out of their present, if at all. Josie has been writing since fourth or fifth grade, in Eloy, when her teacher encouraged the students to create their own stories in response to curriculum materials. "She said we didn't have to, but I would always do it." She still does, from an ongoing need, I believe, to contend with experience, accommodate to it, reconcile with it.

One witnesses the struggle for wholeness—of family, of the human and natural cycles, of self-perception—in her old portfolio. Of the poems that follow, "His Name" and "Home Is Supposed To Be a Comfortable Place" are more confrontational, while "Moonlight" achieves erotic union—"pretty intimate," Josie smiles.

"Home Is Supposed To Be a Comfortable Place" was written about coming out, in high school.

Though Josie has never read Joseph Conrad, she shares an intention with him, when he declared, "My task is…by the power of the written word, to make your hear, to make you feel…above all, to make you see."

As Josie puts it, "One time I remember riding home from Casa Grande, through what you call Death Valley, near Chuichu. Me and Lynette, coming home, we don't talk. Sometimes we do, but most of the time it's quiet. I can still think. I write stuff in my head. Coming up out of the valley, it was dark. It was a full moon but dark. Farther, you could see lights from a village called Jackrabbit. The mountains were there but it looked like they weren't, just silhouettes. If I could go back to that moment, then I could probably write it, and you'd be able to see what I saw. I want you to see it, how beautiful it was. For someone who read it, I want it to be like they were there."

I think even Conrad might admire the sensory immediacy of "City's Voice," written about a high school friend.

Josie wants an audience. "I am going to put all my writings together in a book. Have it published, maybe. I want people to hear me when I'm writing. To know who I am. I want to be out there, known not just by my family and friends, but other people. 'Oh, she's the one who wrote _____.'" She laughs.

She taps an untitled poem. "This isn't finished. It's like it started in the middle. When I write my book, this will be my beginning":

I will stand here as an Indian woman, an American
Indian woman, mind you.
And pound my fist on this podium until you have
realized.
I will pound my fist on this podium like it is the
sacred circle drum of many ceremonies and make
up my own.
I will stand here and pound on this podium until
you have realized, until I have finished
singing my song.
I will stand here and pound on this drum until
I have finished my song.

Attempts to heal the past, to make it whole, don't come
easily. Josie seems to have forgiven the nameless stepfather of "His
Name," who was shot and killed two years ago. "I felt sorry for
him. Somebody must have done something to him when he was
young, and that's why he was the way he was." (Josie's birth father
was "a Mexican guy my mom didn't really know. I didn't really
care. It doesn't matter. I'm here.")

The relationship with Lucilda, her foster mother, may
have reached a truce. While once they didn't speak for a year, "We
talked about it and kind of laughed about it."

Obviously, Josie grieves the fate of her sister Connie, her
runaway partner from childhood. For a time, she invited Connie
to live in Covered Wells, "but we had a lot of problems. I was
trying to help her, but it seems like she was damaged already.

"She's still with that guy. She married him. She has six
kids, all from that guy." He beats her; his family steals her food
stamps; they borrowed her car and wrecked it.

"It's sad she had to grow up like she did. She stayed on
the run until she turned eighteen. She didn't finish school. She
can't get a job now because she doesn't have her GED. She's really
struggling. I told her, 'If you'd gone back with me to the Girls'
Home, none of this would have happened.'"

The mother in Josie's life remains little more than letters composed in her head, unsent. "I don't even know her. It's like we just barely met. Just this year, because I was working with Child Welfare, I found out how it all works." Josie's voice shakes. "When I was in the Girls' Home, the foster home, all she had to do was take classes, go to a rehab center, and then she could have come and got me. Any time, she could have done that. And she didn't. She never did."

Home, at last, in the village where her lover was raised, the house built by that family's own hands, Josie understands as few could the vulnerability of happiness, its transience. "Yeah, it is scary." She laughs. "It seemed when I was growing up, every time something was going kind of good, there was always something there to come along and mess it up. It would be like, 'This is happening, thank God,' and all of a sudden, bam! You'd trip and fall so hard on your face. That's how it was. I'm trying not to be *too* happy."

# His Name

I remember this man: I can't remember his
name.
He steered my mom's boat with all of us,
her kids, like he had no shame.
Pulling us down the mountain, my mom tried
to keep us steady, she even tried going against
the rapid parts.
He eventually took over, we continued to sail
lower and lower, sunken hearts.
Sometimes he was okay, sometimes he was
sad, sometimes he was weird, but mostly
he was mad.
I would think to myself, "God, mom, how
stupid can you be, why do you let him treat
you so bad."
What was his name?
Still I hated it, but things remained the same.
Mom would take beatings so bad, he tried to
kill her, wanted to make it look like a drowning.
He carried us from state to state to town to
town from morning to morning.
I still can't remember his name!
Although I think he's the one to blame.
The water was dirty with filth, needles,
beer cans and bottles, nothing but trash.
My mom no longer looked like Miss T.O.*
He did it, stripped her of her sash.
And the water, the rapids, the states, the
towns, the mornings, and the water, it ran.
We sailed high and low carried by what's his
name, this man.
I can't remember his name, what's his

name. I can't remember his name, but
I remember the shame and blame the main
thing.
My father, my father, no name, but my
father who ran like the river.

*—Josie Frye, 1997*

*Miss Tohono O'odham

# Moonlight

I lay awake, restless, wanting, needing
remembered that night      that night
when we stood staring at each other's bodies
only exploring with our eyes
remembered that night      that night
when you turned the light out and let
the shade up.
I remembered looking out the window
and seeing the moon so bright and beautiful
turning the wild ones in us loose as we
touched and bathed in the moon's light
remembered that night      that night
when I felt you inside me for the first
time
remembered that night      that night
when you explored me inside and out
when I explored you.
I remembered you feeling me and me
feeling pleasure then pain for a moment
letting out a little moan      you covered
my mouth with yours
remembered that night      that night
when we became one with the bed and
let the sheets swallow us whole
remembered that night      that night
when we made love to each other.

—*Josie Frye, 2004*

# Home Is Supposed To Be a Comfortable Place

Where you go after work or school,
  i come home and feel like the
  strangest of all strangers.
Where you go and look in the closet for
  a comfortable pair of clothes to wear
  i come home and look in the closet
    and see myself in all the outfits
    that don't fit.
Where you go and get support, approval,
  and praise
  i come home and get criticized about
    my goals, and i can't wear that one
    outfit that lets me be who i truly am.
Where you go people know who you are and
  try to understand.
  i come home, put on that uncomfortable outfit,
  sweep the dust under the rug, and throw
  all the dirty laundry in the closet, to keep my
  room looking for my parents' approval,
  and straight.

—*Josie Frye, 2007*

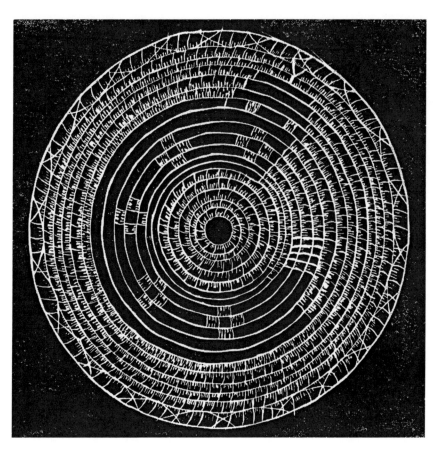

—*Dionne Lopez*

# MARVIN LEWIS, JR.


Marvin Lewis, Jr., was born and raised, and still lives, in Topawa, eight miles south of Sells, on the Tohono O'odham Nation.

# Loving

Love is like a red
rose blooming in
the hot summer. When
the buds come it's
just like the first
time you see her.
When the rose starts
blooming it's just like
you're getting to know
her. When the rose
is finished blooming
you really know
her. The thorns are
like a bad thing
that happens with
her. When the rose
dies you can
become white birds.

*—Marvin Lewis, Jr., 8ᵗʰ Grade*

# The Memories

It happened one night when I was lying on my fluffy bed in the dark. I was lying there thinking about my cousin's death. I just so happened to move my curtain and looked out to see the stars. The stars reminded me of all the things we had done together. As I was looking out the window, I started visualizing the way we put him to eternal rest, going down in the hole. I didn't know I was crying until one of my family members turned on the outside light where my room's window is. I blinked my eyes. I kept on looking out the window.

As I saw the stars, I also saw a black object sitting on the window sill. My eyes were not focused to the light to see the object. My eyes started getting focused and I started seeing a shaded brown and black. Then I knew what I was looking at was an owl. It looked so cool that I didn't tell anyone about it. My cousin is still with me in his own world.

*—Marvin Lewis, Jr., 9th Grade*

# Indian Animals

There are different
kinds of animals
coming together to
become a tribe.
As they come they
hear beating of a
drum that brings
the wildness out
of them. They all
start dancing different ways.
Showing their moves
to the other animals.
As the coyote's
paws hit the
ground it sounds
like thunder. As
the eagle flies
above their heads
it leaves the
winter winds.

*—Marvin Lewis, Jr., 9th Grade*

# A Giving Heart

There is a woman who looks so good in a dress or in jeans. She is tall, plays basketball. Long hair that looks like falling stars that are bright. The woman gives her heart away. She gives it to a boy who she did not know.

The woman meets the boy one night on the basketball courts. She likes the way he moves with the ball. He is about ten years old. He is a boy that is big and tall for his age. He is fast like a deer running away from its enemy. She gives this boy her heart because she would like the boy to be her lover, but she is too old for him.

The boy keeps the heart with his heart. This is because no one gave him anything in his life.

*—Marvin Lewis, Jr., 10th Grade*

# The Day Is Bright Light

The day is coming with a
warm light. Rising over
the spirit mountain. When I
look at it I see our Nation's
colors, of our flag. Yellow is
the light of the sun.
Purple is the shadow of
the mountain. Feathers falling
from the eagle as it soars
over the sacred mountain.
So they can be used in
the spiritual way of life.

*—Marvin Lewis, Jr., 10ᵗʰ Grade*

# Because

Roses are red
my eyes are blue
too much staring at you
because you are wearing
a white velvet dress in the
light of the moon
with your legs smooth
like a newborn baby
hair shinier than a
diamond in the sunlight.

*—Marvin Lewis, 11ᵗʰ Grade*

# Night, Morning

Day is ending.
Night is coming.
Night is
a room without windows
with the lights off.
Animals run in
groups, fearing
the night man
that walks
the desert.

You rise up to see the morning
I wait for you, I get up
before you. I watch you get up
like my own child. You
let me see your beautiful color
that warms up my day.
You rise over the beautiful mountain
in the Tohono O'odham land.

*—Marvin Lewis, 11th Grade*

◎  ◎  ◎  ◎  ◎  ◎

I still think of Marvin Lewis as ArtsReach's greatest unpublished poet. Four consecutive years I submitted his work to four different guest editors of *Dancing with the Wind*. Not one piece was chosen.

Marvin never seemed to care, but I was puzzled and frustrated for him. Years later, I brood over these and other omissions of deserving students, long after they themselves, I suspect, have forgotten they ever wrote the stuff. It's almost as painful as receiving a rejection of my own.

Of course another reader couldn't be expected to share my tastes, but did no one else appreciate the way the careful construction of the rose metaphor in "Loving" releases into those white birds? What about the touching "Memories," with the blunt horror of Marvin's cousin "going down in the hole"? Aren't we intrigued and troubled by a grown woman falling in love with a ten-year-old in "A Giving Heart," only to lose our breath at the amazing turn the story takes in its final sentence?

I can't pretend to be objective.

Shy, modest, and very busy, Marvin proved almost as elusive an interview as Josie Frye. Determined that these written relics of his past finally would have an audience, I dogged him for a year and a half between our first and second sessions.

On the day of our first talk, June '07, the temperature hits 109. I skim through browned-out desert toward the tribal jail in Sells, where the Love Poet, as I'd always thought of Marvin, labors as a guard, overseeing his neighbors and sometimes former classmates in their orange prison pants.

Across the road, a man washes his horse as he might a car, circling the motionless animal with a hose, the dappled coat glistening.

The room where we'd planned to meet is unavailable, so we stand outdoors for an hour or so under the shade of an overhang. Marvin's two children, Cyndi, seven, and Angelo, two, circle and surge around us throughout. Inmates pass to and fro. It's not a setting conducive to discussing romance, but I try.

Marvin really *was* a romantic, "Loving" an eighth-grade fantasy concocted out of pure yearning. But by eleventh grade, "Because" had an object for its desire.

"Yeah! Love was an idea that happened," Marvin says. He and Diane Vieyra married in 1999, while still in high school. She works for the tribal Water Authority, in well maintenance.

His responses are brief, a reticence enlivened by a quick smile or chuckle. I recall vividly his tentative writing habits in the past, the need for encouragement and even prodding, then the startling leaps and resolutions that would appear on the page. Burlier now, a thick braid to his waist, he seems to have subsumed those darting inquiries into the role of responsible family man. Tattoos cover his arms, but they are the names of his children.

Marvin has settled into his role as a detention officer, mastering multiple duties. "I'm not too sure yet if this is something I'll go on with. It's just something my wife—well, she didn't make me, but we talked about my applying. It's a steady job. I know it's always going to be here," he laughs.

His grace and low-key humor may help defuse the inevitable awkwardness. "I know a lot of people who come through," he says. "At first they were embarrassed. Then they got to know what I do, they went along with it. When they get out, some of them say hi, some of them run and hide."

Marvin grows wistful remembering his grandmother's cattle. "I was interested in it. In school my favorite classes were Vo Ag, the cattle, driving tractors. I used to work with livestock." Since his grandmother's death, Marvin and his father have tried to determine if she still owned a herd. "So far we haven't heard anything. We thought about finding some and starting up again."

Despite Marvin's distinctive writing, and the heartfelt appreciation of *himdag* that runs though it, he makes no large claims for himself in either case.

"I try to write, but I end up throwing it out. Just random things that come." To my relief, he does remember publishing a poem, not in *Dancing with the Wind* but in *Red Ink*, produced by the University of Arizona's American Indian Studies. So he wasn't shut out completely.

"I believe in my culture and I try to teach my kids," he says. "My daughter wants to be an O'odham singer. She's trying to speak O'odham. I try to talk to her. I speak somewhat, not too well. I can understand it more than speak it."

If Marvin downplays his accomplishments, he has a vocal advocate in Cyndi, his seven-year-old daughter.

"My dad cooks meat outside. He cooks it and flips it over. I help him cook eggs in the morning, or sausage.

"Sometimes I write with my dad.

"A lot of times my dad takes me to the park when he's off work.

"Sometimes my dad makes a rattle (*shawikud*). He made one for me."

Marvin acknowledges this. "I had a friend paint it. I used to sing," he adds. "I don't remember the songs too well."

"He sings, though," Cyndi insists. "When I was five years old he used to sing songs to me because sometimes I don't want to get bad dreams. Then I started going to sleep when he was almost done."

"Cyndi is not shy," Marvin points out. "She's very outgoing."

In fact, Cyndi takes over the remainder of the interview. She seems to have the gift of total recall—a rock 'n' roll party featuring her cousin, trips to Mexico and around the state, her afterschool activities, the painted *shawikud*. A sample:

"I read in school. I used to be homeschooled. Then I went to kindergarten. I won an award in kindergarten and I won an award in first grade. I had an award for being quiet and an award for helping people. Sometimes the teacher puts a star on my writing. Sometimes she puts a heart on it. My grandma told me to keep writing. My teacher is Miss Perry. She is Miss Mayer's sister. Miss Mayer used to be my mom's teacher. Sometimes Miss Mayer has to go through a lot. Miss Perry, too. 'Cause we don't pay attention. I pay attention. I can help people. I teach my friend writing because she doesn't remember. My friend always plays around. She keeps talking, and Miss Perry has to yell at her. She's always in detention. She's expelled because she did something in the hall. Last time she was doing something in the bathroom. Someone caught her playing around. She always gets in trouble. She was expelled for three days. Now she's expelled for a lot of days."

When I next see Marvin, I hear the children's voices intermittently from inside the house as we stand outdoors, leaning against his car, the tape recorder between us. Marvin has a heavy cold and, typically for his current schedule, has slept between two and three hours. It's a balmy December day, 2008, mesquite tossing in the breeze. The Baboquivari Mountains lie straight across the valley, the twisted majesty of *Waw Giwulk* rising from their midst. It's the same view Marvin envisioned in his high school poems, because he's living in the same lone tract home, solid brown block, as then. His parents' roof is visible a quarter mile away, through desert shrubbery.

Graveyard shift? Arriving home at 7:30 a.m., passing kisses to departing wife and Cyndi, crashing a couple of hours until son Angelo wakes for breakfast, minding him until a brief afternoon nap…it's all the same to Marvin. "To me day or night doesn't matter, long as I work. Graveyard is quiet. At night you can get more things done that need to be done."

A year and a half before, when I'd asked if Marvin was doing what he'd always wanted to, he laughed dismissively. "Not my job!" Within the chill of recession, perhaps, his appreciation has warmed. "I like it," he says now. "It's different every day. I know all the shifts, so I don't really care which shift I go to."

Work has silenced the Love Poet, Marvin admits. He no longer writes Diane poems. "Work kinds of drains me out," he says.

So has adulthood altered his vision of love itself?

"To me it seems like it didn't change. It's still the same. We've got more love to share. We have the two kids with us. Everywhere we go," he adds, laughing. "They're always with us. Even now, around Christmas time, it's hard to get their presents because they're always with us."

Would he write Diane a poem now?

"Yeah, I'll try it."

# Guardian Angel

She cares about everyone in her life
like a guardian angel. She shows more
love to our kids than a mother.
Her love grows like a plant. She
plants her seeds into our kids so they
can be strong and bright like their mother,
as I call her, their guardian angel.
The guardian angel is beautiful
as a silk rose. Her strength
is brighter than the sun, so no one can burn
her out.
This is why I love her.

*—Marvin Lewis, Jr., 2009*

*—Robert Arredondo*

## YOLANDA DARRELL

After eight years in Tucson, Yolanda Darrell, Tohono O'odham, has returned to her childhood home in Sells, on the Tohono O'odham Nation.

# Angel

He did not cry,
he did not smile.
His eyes didn't open
even for a little while.

He was just a baby
not yet born.
His mother's heart was happy
and then it was torn.

They named him Angel
and laid him down to sleep
But him in their hearts
they will always keep.

*In loving memory of Angel Emory Johnson-Ramon*

*—Yolanda Darrell, 8th Grade*

# Sunrise

I sit on my porch wrapped in my
blanket, waiting for the new day
to peek over the mountain tops.
The sky slowly changing from dark
to light.
The stars seem to fade like the
memory of an aging man.
I close my eyes and hear the magic
of life all around me,
the soft whistling of the morning breeze
the singing of crickets and the mysterious laughter
of coyote.
Suddenly there is silence.
An old song drifts to mind.
I sing and welcome the new day
as the sun's smile rises.

—*Yolanda Darrell, 11th Grade*

# The Fancy Shawl Dancer

Rose was a beautiful, tall and very slim seventeen-year-old girl. She enjoyed many things like school, singing, and dancing. She had just started fancy shawl dancing, and she liked it very much. She began traveling to pow-wows with her family and eventually started competing.

A few months after she started traveling, she was given an eagle plume to wear when she danced. The elderly man who gave it to her explained the importance and meaning of it. She was told to keep it covered and in a safe place when it was not worn. When it was being worn, it had to be tightly pinned in her hair so it wouldn't fall off in the arena. If it falls, she would be punished.

She told the elder man that she understood the respect for the eagle plume and the pow-wow circle, so she would take good care of it. And she did.

She became an excellent fancy shawl dancer. She won a lot of competitions with her graceful footwork and rhythm. Her spirit seemed to dance with the beat of the drum. Everyone respected her and enjoyed watching her.

About a year after she received the eagle plume, she became careless. She was at the Gathering of Nations Pow-wow, the biggest pow-wow in North America. She was getting ready for her competition. Her mother told her to double check her outfit and feather to make sure they were secure. She ignored her mother's advice, and said everything would be fine.

While she was dancing in her competition, her plume fell to the floor of the arena. She stopped and stood there. An elderly lady came out to the arena and picked it up. This usually happens when a feather is dropped. She picked it up and looked at Rose and said, "You have shown here today that you do not respect our sacred eagle. Now I must take this plume from you and it will be given to someone who will respect and care for it." Then the old lady slowly turned and walked away.

Rose walked out of the arena with her head hanging and tears in her eyes. No one looked at her the same, and her talent seemed to disappear. She was no longer highly respected by the people in the pow-wow circle. When she realized this, she never set foot in another pow-wow arena. Now, whenever someone mentions pow-wow, she cries because there is a hole in her heart that only her dancing could fill.

*—Yolanda Darrell, 11th Grade*

## Their Souls Dance to a Different Beat

She does homework and gets straight A's
He's been kicked out twice
She loves poetry and sees the beauty in nature
He likes the words in his heavy metal music
    and his art is in his tattoos.
She is surrounded by her family while
He's locked in his little empty box
She says her prayers and counts her blessings
He curses at the sky for his failures
Their souls dance to a different beat
    but still their hearts beat as one.

*—Yolanda Darrell, 12th Grade*

⊚  ⊚  ⊚  ⊚  ⊚  ⊚

Yolanda Darrell has an iconic sort of face, straight black hair swept back simply, a firm nose and chin suggesting purpose, brightened by an incipient smile and shadowed by her sad eyes.

Perhaps I'm reading too much into her features, knowing the qualities that I attribute to them.

But Yolanda must have seemed larger than life to her friend Sonja Blackowl back in eighth grade, when Sonja wrote this poem:

### An Indian Girl

There's a girl named Yolanda.
When Yolanda dances
the wind blows in her
hair. Hair as black as the
eagle's feather. Her glasses
shining like a crystal off a rock.
She walks straight as
an arrow and proudly. When she
dances, she dances like an eagle
flying and watching over the
people. She dances like one of
the ghosts. She has the world at
her feet. Everyone follows her,
she's like a guide the way she
turns, as if the world turns
faster when the music plays. She
dances to the beat like a rabbit
leaping across the desert.

"Dancing was like my church. That's where I did my

prayers. It was my release," Yolanda says now.

But by high school, when Yolanda wrote "The Fancy Shawl Dancer," dancing already was tinged with loss. "I was struggling because I had lost my grandpa, a lot of losses. It was like one after another after another. For a year I was supposed to stay out of the pow-wow circle, because that's a mourning period. I couldn't get back to it. Once the year was getting close, something else happened." She hasn't danced pow-wow since.

I knew some facts about Yolanda because her auntie Sharon lives down the street from me, in northwest Tucson. Yolanda's mother had died several years ago. Valedictorian of her middle school, ranked third in her high school graduating class, Yolanda had dropped out of college. And in April of this year, 2008, Sharon had rung my doorbell to tell me Yolanda's father had died. The memorial service was my first glimpse of Yolanda since high school, wrapped in black, shining with tears.

I also knew that Yolanda worked in an elder-care facility, and I had a theory about this. You'd think I would have learned by now, but I can't help myself. It was a theory of exile from grief and failure, surrounded by human decline and death.

"I love it," Yolanda says about her job of four years. "These people are full of life. It's resort-style living. They do a lot of outings. They have clubs, a bridge club, a drama club. They do bingo. They have Red Hatters, a social group for elderly women. They wear purple shirts and red hats. They have good food. Yeah! Kind of like an adult camp." She laughs. "They call me the multitasker because I've done every job there except for housekeeping and maintenance. No matter what I'm doing there, I enjoy it."

No mistake, five months after the death of Willard "Half" Darrell, his house in Sells, Yolanda's old/new home, is a carnival. Sunlight streams in on walls so densely packed with smiling family photos that they might be tiles. Wearing a flashy red top, Yolanda fires quips and barbs at her brother Martin, perched on the opposite couch, wheelchair at the ready. He responds in kind.

His home caregiver, Maylene, joins in. Laughter erupts frequently.

Much of Yolanda's happy childhood was spent in that house, beginning in fourth grade. A modest tract home, beige stucco, it later was expanded to accommodate Martin's disability. He was born with spina bifida.

Yolanda can remember stepping off the school bus, greeted by the aroma of her mother Cindy's banana bread. Baking side by side, they'd become so absorbed in talking that "our hands would move by themselves. I liked just being together. My mother was a very beautiful woman, inside and out. She had a smile for everyone."

Yolanda's father, the joker, would play hide-and-seek in clothing racks when the family shopped in Tucson. "He was just like a little kid. We'd be looking for him. Mom would say, 'Stop it, you're embarrassing me.'

"I got maybe in junior high when I found out my Dad's name wasn't Half," Yolanda laughs. "Everybody knows him as Half. Growing up, he was the youngest of seven children, and he was a short boy, so they called him Half-Pint. Once he hit puberty and shot up, they just shortened it to Half.

"He was a heavy equipment operator. He worked with the big dozers, the dikes and the dams, the water conservation around the rez. I used to listen to him talk about it, straight-edging with the blade along the dirt. He watched other people do it. I'd tell him, 'It's like an art to you, Dad.'

"He said, 'Yeah. I take pride in every little detail.'"

Until the day of her death, Cindy Darrell was a "very, very strong woman. She was working three jobs at one time, Basha's, the bank, housing. She had me at a young age. She had my brother with his condition, and she still took care of us the best way she could. She never drank, never did drugs, she was always home with us. Her family was her life.

"Even when we found out she had cancer, she didn't believe it. She said, 'I'm not sick. I don't feel sick.' She fought it out until that last month, when it really took her."

Cindy Darrell resisted the hospital until "she was gasping for air." Yolanda says. "She sat there waiting for the ambulance, balancing her checkbook, so we knew exactly what we had, making sure we'd be OK."

I tell Yolanda I find great decisiveness in her writing, the way "The Fancy Shawl Dancer" briskly propels the reader through the essentials, ending with the terse, evocative "hole in her heart that only her dancing could fill," or the deft parallelism in "Their Souls Dance to a Different Beat." There's the remarkable simile in "Sunrise," where "The stars seem to fade like the memory of an aging man."

This, too, was rooted in her childhood. "I spent a lot of time in my room. When I wasn't reading, I was writing. I kept a journal of thoughts in my head, and poems. My parents used to beg me, 'Come out! Watch TV with us! Come out and talk with us!'"

A top student, outgoing, Yolanda was active in pow-wow dancing and varsity basketball. She traveled to Australia to play volleyball (funded by Cindy Darrell's banana bread), and to Washington, D.C., with her government teacher, to lobby Congress.

The blow fell when she entered the University of Arizona just months after graduating Baboquivari High.

"I wasn't prepared at all. The things they taught us here weren't up to Tucson standards. I took pre-calculus here, but when I went to the U of A I tested into pre-algebra. It made me frustrated. I kept thinking, I can handle this, I can do this…

"It was frustrating," she repeats. "In high school I fought with the school board. I was the only student on a committee with the Superintendent. He got to know me very well. By my junior year I had taken all the math they had to offer. I was worried because I was going to miss out on the whole year. They considered doing satellite classes through Pima College, but that never happened. I used to tell them, am I going to be prepared? I was serious about school. That was frustrating," she says a third time.

"Our dropout rate was high. I know it was because it wasn't challenging enough. A lot of the students got bored."

Leaving the U of A, Yolanda enrolled at Pima, but then her mother's illness intervened, and she never went back.

"I took it hard when I lost my Mom. I got lost there for a couple of years. Soul-searching, questioning my life, being angry with God for having her go through all that, after everything she'd done her whole life, and having her suffer that way. Angry and hurt. Bouncing from job to job."

Her misery found company, a tight band of friends all reeling from the loss of loved ones, clinging together, hanging out. Eventually they shared a house. "We'd laugh together, we'd cry together." I'm reminded of the Onion Cellar, the club in Gunter Grass's novel *The Tin Drum*, where post-war survivors gathered to peel onions and weep. But Yolanda insists on the lightness. "Anybody was upset, we'd flip it around, always joking, always making fun of each other."

Briefly, with other companions, she slipped into riskier behavior, drinking and drugs. "Acting, not paying attention to consequences. There was one car accident that scared me."

Finally she "got bored. I wanted to do something productive with myself. I needed to kick myself in the butt."

The kick landed her at the retirement community. A resident, impressed with her temp job typing his poetry manuscript, fetched her an application, talking her up at the office. Yolanda immediately submitted it, and was hired the next day.

While she questions, "Is this what I want to be doing permanently?" for now Yolanda is fulfilled.

It's the people. The residents "all have their own stories." There's the couple who trade ailments. "One gets out of the hospital, the other one goes into the hospital. They don't get angry or sad. I've never seen them mad at each other. They're always joking like they're teenagers, like their relationship is still new. It's cute."

Another resident has adopted her. "I was serving in the dining room, and I saw her on a daily basis. She asked about my family and I told her where I was from. She says, 'No. Your family's too far. You're my daughter now.' So now she calls me her daughter and I call her Mom. She was a music teacher. She's got an amazing spirit. There's a light around this woman."

Her companion was the poet, who left Yolanda handmade books before he died.

"We deal with the loss and sickness," she says. "My dad used to say, 'Isn't it hard?' I said, 'Yeah, but if they've been sick for a while, it's kind of a blessing. Just like with my Mom, I didn't want to lose my Mom, but I remember toward the end I prayed to God, 'Just take her,' because I didn't like seeing her suffer any more."

Her eight years in Tucson "urbanized" her, Yolanda reflects. Her father used to ask, "When are you coming back to God's country?"

In fact, even before his death she was planning to do just that. Though she had no intimation Half might be ill, perhaps he did. She remembers him asking, "If anything happened to me, would you come home to be with your brother?" She told him, "Of course, Dad."

"Just come home. I want you here. I want you to move back with us," he said

Yolanda agreed, once her lease expired in June. But April 8, the night after the NCAA basketball championship, Martin remembers, Half died in his sleep. Strangely fitting, considering he had played, Yolanda played; even Martin played against University of Arizona greats Richard Jefferson and Gilbert Arenas in the annual Lame for a Game charity exhibition.

"My dad *was* basketball," Yolanda says. That week they'd been joking and teasing over the Final Four, their rival teams, by phone. "It was just him laughing. Whenever I'd call, whoever was there, he'd pass the phone around the room. 'Here. Talk to 'Landa.'"

Her natural vivacity falls still when she speaks of her

parents, the underlying rhythm of this conversation. Her pensive eyes fill in the spaces.

"Even after my Mom was gone, my Dad still…That's what helps me, knowing he's gone, I know they're still together, and he's OK now, because he missed her so much. He missed her so much."

Crisis may have played its role in Yolanda's evolving spirituality. Raised in both Christian and traditional ways, she says now, "I know my Creator. But I don't go to church. I believe in the traditional, I'itoi. I have a strong belief in the traditional because I know it works. I used to get sick when I was younger. The hospital said, 'There's nothing wrong with her.' But I would be sick. My grandma would take me to the medicine man, and he'd fix me.

"I look at the Bible as a history book. There's lessons to be learned there, but I think it's kind of a scare tactic—'oh, this is going to happen if I don't do that.' I believe that Jesus lived. But I don't think he's still here, or he's coming back. Maybe he was God, or maybe it was people's point of view, how they saw things at the time."

Our interview has not run out of surprises for me. I presume to ask Yolanda if she had ever found a love, someone her own age, to relieve the ache of loss.

"Mm-hmm."

Do you have that going on?

"Yes. That keeps me going."

Down here?

"Yes."

Has that been going on for a while?

"Six years."

When you were living in town, were you able to see him on a regular basis?

"Her."

Unlike Josie Frye, Yolanda had not always loved women. Another contributor to the "lost period" was a three-year relationship with a man who "did me wrong." But with Emmylyne

Jose, a childhood friend, "it just happened. She's somebody I clicked with. I get a lot of encouragement and a lot of love.

"In a lot of ways, she found me and brought me back. She reminded me of who I was, because I was losing that. She gave me strength to be myself. When I was growing up here I was constantly worried about what people thought of me. Part of the reason I did so well in school is that I was driven—I've got to prove myself. Now, who cares what they think? I'm happy, and I'm me, just getting through the days.

"I've never experienced anything so true. I've come across a lot of fake people in my life, and when you find something real, you want to hang on to it."

Despite the hardships in Yolanda's young life, self-pity is foreign to her. About her parents' early deaths, she says, "I was lucky. I had great parents." Assuming the responsibility for Martin's care is no burden; she treasures him as "all I've got left" of her happy family. Cleaning the house is "a stress reliever." The daily commute to southside Tucson—"I've known that road most of my life. Every time I drive it, it seems to get shorter."

The rollicking atmosphere at Club Darrell apparently is the norm. "Right after we buried my dad, my cousin was here, and somebody had stopped by to see him. We were in here laughing about my dad, talking about each other, making fun, laughing pretty loud. My cousin came and said, 'I told my friend that you just buried your dad, we just buried my uncle. The guy is looking at me weird and says, 'It doesn't sound like it.'"

Half, who grew to embrace Emmylyne—Emmy—too, would approve. Or, as Yolanda sees it, he *does* approve. When I ask what has replaced dancing as her church, she doesn't hesitate. "My prayer is talking to my Mom. Talking to my Dad."

Yolanda and Emmy share the bedroom where Yolanda grew up. Her parents' room, meanwhile, persists intact. Her mother's clothes hang in the closet, above her shoes. Her jewelry is there. "One day my Dad said, 'I guess I've got to do something about those shoes.' That was five years ago. He never did.

"It's their room. I go in and talk to them. I lie down on the bed, like I used to, my head in my Mom's lap. I'd talk to her, or listen to my Mom and Dad.

"The other night Emmy and I were in our room. 'What's that?' We heard their voices. We heard them talking."

My second conversation with Yolanda, two weeks later, turns to writing itself, the unpredictable potency of specific detail, and at its close I ask, "Can we try a piece of writing today?"

"OK," she says, in an uncharacteristically small voice. Her poem is inspired by the comings and goings of her four-year-old niece, Leilani. Instinctively it finds an organizing argument, a dialogue between childhood's happy obliviousness and the adult's apprehensiveness of pain. Yolanda scrutinizes the draft sternly, crosses out, touches up, accepts an ending, and re-writes—her first poem in seven years.

# Leilani

Little girl running carefree
barefoot in the desert.
No worries about the small
critters or sharp hot rocks
under her feet.
Skipping, hopping and flying
free. Lost in her own little
adventure.
"Don't wander too far...
Be careful, Leilani.
I don't want you to get hurt."
She doesn't hear, she
doesn't watch her step.
She's just a little girl
enjoying her little life.
She's fearless.
She's curious.
She grabs a hold of
the tree branch and does a flip
in one quick motion.
Her hair swings like it will get caught
in the tree.
She's a beautiful free spirit
ambitious and smart.
I worry and watch
my little sponge soaking
up life. She'll learn.

—*Yolanda Darrell, 2008*

—*Lorianne Narcho*

# WENONA ORTEGAS
## (1977-2005)

Wenona Ortegas lived in the Sells and Chukud Kuk Districts of the Tohono O'odham Nation. She died on her birthday, September 24, in a car crash that also killed her sister Tanya Segundo.

# The O'odham War

I was in my room. As I was spacing out on the mirror, thinking of old Indian legends and fights, I fell and suddenly I was sitting on a little hill spaced out on a rock.

I realized I was 100 years back in time, in the middle of a war between the Apaches and the O'odham. I got hit in the head by a rock and passed out.

When I came to, I was lying down in a little adobe. Boy, did my head hurt, like a spear going into a heart of an evil person and all their powers releasing. I opened my eyes. I saw an old woman. It was one of my ancestors. I could tell by the way she was dressed, with her long hair, long dress, and no shoes. I said, "Where am I?"

She looked startled. She got a rock and threw it at me. That's when I knew she didn't know I was an O'odham, 'cause of my jeans, black T-shirt, and Vision shoes. The rock felt weird. It got my arm numb. I said, "Lady, what's up with you?" But then I came to realize that she didn't know English. Once again she threw a rock, and continued to.

After the tenth rock I was in my room looking in the mirror. I guess I'm just thinking too hard.

—*Wenona Ortegas, 6<sup>th</sup> Grade*

# The Killing

I had a dream that I went back, far back in time. It felt like I was sinking down, down to the bottom of the sea and drowning at the same time. I couldn't breathe. Then I hit down onto the hard surface of the Earth.

And guess where I was. In South Dakota with the Sioux Indians, of course. Just going into battle with Custer and his men. I figured that since Sioux are Indians and I am, too, that it should be my duty to fight for the Indian land. And kill at least one of the enemy.

So I went into battle with my black horse, spear, and my bow and arrow. I saw Custer with a worried look on his red, pinkish face, looking around as scared as hell. And blond hair with his blue uniform. I pointed my arrow to Custer, and killed him from long distance. The killing of him was like a great Indian spirit coming to life once more.

Then one of Custer's men killed me from long distance with his gun. I looked towards the man as he pointed the gun my way. I paid no attention. I was rejoicing over the death of Custer. Suddenly I was dead!

I woke up and was holding a feather. Then I said to myself, "An Indian never dies, because their spirit never dies in reality."

*—Wenona Ortegas, 5th Grade*

# Great Spirits

Jade was a young man, and as a child his
grandparents had told him that one day he was to fulfill
the dreams of the great spirits. Before the beginning of
the winter season, the people of the village had a big
ceremony to get Jade prepared for his journey.
As the morning of the beginning of the first
winter day was ending, the elderly of the village stood
around Jade and sang a song.
This was the first night of winter. It was cold.
The thick fog filled the air, and darkness filled the mind
of anyone who thought, for that was all you could see
on that mountain. Which was high, with snow on the
ground, trees that led to the great spirits' world, and
cliffs that led to hell, with endless pits, hopeless cries,
and a helpless death.
Jade was walking on the mountain. He was five
feet from the top, when a dark shadow appeared in front
of him. It looked helplessly at Jade as if the dark shadow
had visions in its eyes but wasn't able to act on them.
The dark shadow just stood in front of Jade and then
moved.
Jade's reason for coming to this particular
mountain, to stay for three days and three nights, was
because it was time for him to carry out the great spirits'
dreams, and this mountain held those dreams, along
with death.
As he got to the top, other dark shadows
appeared. They called him by his Indian name, "Shining
Sun," so he knew they were old, wise relatives who
had passed on. He didn't let them know he saw their
presence, and felt the sense to talk to them, knowing
they would bring death to him.

He sat down on the peak of the mountain, gazing into the fog and all the darkness appearing in front of him, calling and touching, motioning for him to come join them in death.

Jade knew he had to resist their call from death. He also knew he had to be strong and wise to gain his powers to heal the sick and bring peace to the disturbed. So as he sat, he meditated, thinking of all the things he must resist, such as his relatives and their words.

After meditating, he prayed to our precious grandfathers above, asking for mental, physical, spiritual and emotional growth, along with wholeness, nourishment, and protection.

Until those other two days were up, he continued this. When those three days were up, he was as symbolic as the sun, filled with wholeness and spirit to be alive, knowing he had resisted the temptation of evil and was now a medicine man.

—*Wenona Ortegas, 7ᵗʰ Grade*

# The Journey

I was walking one day on the hills in the desert, feeling empty and missing my father, who had passed away, who had gone on to the spirit world, not really understanding why, only knowing that I guess it was his time to go on and there are certain things that happen in a person's life that they may not always understand.

I stopped walking and sat down amongst the earth, rocks, sky and sun. I looked around, and everything was a daze, like an unsure dream of not knowing who I was, where I was going, or whether I could go on.

As I turned, feeling dazed, hills that were recognizable to me were like strangers who I was eager to meet but was unsure of their reaction. From the hills appeared one of the most beautiful sunsets you can imagine, and along with that an old woman who was motioning for me to come, come and join her. So I walked toward her with a feeling of no fear. Things seemed to change in ways that are indescribable, puzzling and unreal like a dream.

I got to the old woman and she said, "It is time for you to take a journey to see your dad. It will only be for a short time, but it will be long enough for the memories to last a lifetime."

As I journeyed to Death, I could see many people, spirits, beings having a good time. I could hear people laughing like they were never going to laugh again and they were enjoying it while they had the chance. I was welcomed by many of my relatives, my ancestors, and my father. He hugged me the way he always had and said, "Hello, my girl, I missed you."

I said, "Daddy, I missed you so much that it's been

driving me crazy. I don't understand, Dad." I hugged him tighter than I ever had, not wanting to let him go, knowing I had only a short time with my father until it is time for me to go on.

—*Wenona Ortegas, 9th Grade*

# Free

As I stand here
The only rain that falls
From any part of the sky
Are the tears from my eyes.
My tears leave
A drip imprint
In the soft piled earth
That has been specially laid
To shelter
You.
The fragrance
Of freshly prepared flowers
Enhances my memories
I had forgotten,
And memories
I had wanted to forget.
My thoughts were not
Of joy
But of death.
If only I had gone
Instead of you
To the Dreaming
Place
Would I have
Freshly prepared flowers
Along with my shelter,
Would it even matter?
I kneel
Gracefully
As if I were dancing
Honoring and respecting
Mother Earth.

I ask why?
And say
"I miss you."
I want to
Be wrapped
In the earth.
I want to
Let freshly prepared flowers
Warm me
During the times
I need it.
I want to
Be a spirit
Of the great
Ones.
I want to be free.

*—Wenona Ortegas, 10th Grade*

# Covered in Mud

I was thrown in the pool
like when I was pushed into
this world.
No one asked me,
and if I knew what I know now
I would have never come out.
When I got out I shook it off
like a dog does when they get all wet,
and just kind of say, "Get it off me,
here, you have it!"
I took one step forward
and slipped in the mud
kind of like a jerk does
when he doesn't know how
to do something or
like a pig who makes
a bed of it because it's in his nature.
Finally I was pulled out
by God
but I didn't know I had
mud in my eyes
so I walked home
getting stiffer and stiffer.
As I got closer to my door,
as I reached for the doorknob,
the door flew right on open.
It was my mom.
She said, "What happened to you?"
"Well, Mom, first I was reborn.
Then I found myself doing dog things
and then I was being a jerk

and then I felt kind of like a pig.
And do you know what?
God pulled me out of the mud."

*—Wenona Ortegas, 12<sup>th</sup> Grade*

# Mom

My mom's goodness
glows from her body
and her eyes sparkle with peace.
She knows how to deal with
the weighted troubles of
the world around her and
compromise with the world
which she has no control over.
My mom's goodness
is what held me tight
when I was young
and sick in the night.
She forgives me when I continuously stray
even when she shouldn't.
Her goodness helps me
understand when I hate the world
because its weight is too heavy.
She once said I couldn't carry the world
on my shoulders. In time I learned this.
But one day, remembering what she
said, I went in a store and there
was a round pillow of the world.
I saw it, ran to it, then called my mom
and said, "Look Mom, now
I CAN CARRY THE WORLD ON MY SHOULDERS."

—*Wenona Ortegas, 12th Grade*

◎  ◎  ◎  ◎  ◎  ◎

From the cemetery at San Miguel, across the border from
Mexico, the southernmost reach of Tohono O'odham land in the
United States, I follow Muriel Segundo's pickup truck north. It's
a rez truck, high, wide, and heavy, and when it abruptly pulls off
the road I follow its diagonal track across dry grass. Muriel parks
beside two wooden crosses, "Wenona" and "Tanya," flanking a
shrine that looks like a tiny, white house.

"This is where Wenona's truck went off," Muriel says. I
realize we have just taken the exact path that killed her daughters,
the vehicle careening from the road, rolling and bouncing across
hard dirt, throwing them from the cab.

"Tanya died instantly. But Wenona—the Border Patrol
and the Rangers got there, and one of the Border Patrol noticed
that she was still breathing. They said she made a movement,
sighed, took a breath, and she was gone."

The sisters were on their way to Tucson to meet Muriel
and the rest of the family for a birthday celebration. Though
the birthday was Wenona's, the belated party would be for her
younger daughter, Wahela. "They had missed her birthday," Muriel
says. That's how Wenona's life had been going recently.

Muriel and her surviving daughter, Rayleen, had been
shopping at Toys R Us when a neighbor phoned. "There was an
accident. We think it's your daughters. I can identify one. That's
Wenona. But I can't recognize the other one. What do you want us
to do? They can take the bodies. They want to make sure that these
are both your daughters."

"No, we're coming," Muriel said. So that is her last
memory of her oldest daughter, Tanya, and her youngest, Wenona,
their bodies torn on the dirt.

Wenona is the empty chair at the table.

I've imagined this death site many times since Mike Harty, Wenona's high school English teacher and mentor, phoned me about the crash. I wanted to ask where it was, but I feared returning to the spot mindlessly, over and over. I could get raw and lost. When Keith Secola sings, in "Indian Car," "We don't get old, we just get younger, when we're flying down the highway, driving in our Indian cars," it's Wenona I hear, eternally young in death.

Having missed the wake, Karen and I staged our own that night, reading aloud all of Wenona's writings over tall glasses of vodka.

I last saw Wenona on her high school graduation night, in 1997. I never knew her as an adult, or her husband, or her two daughters. I met one of them glancingly, visiting a first grade teacher at the primary school in Sells, not long after Wenona's death. The social call was an afterthought, the end of a work day. "This is Deshane, Wenona Ortegas' daughter," the teacher said.

I wanted simply to touch her as something precious, as if doing so would reach across the mortal barrier to her mother.

Unlike Harty, who taught Wenona daily in her freshman and senior years—and for whom she wrote "Covered in Mud"—I know Wenona mostly through her stories and poems.

As a sixth grader she wrote "The O'odham War," a fiercely wistful elegy for a traditional past that doesn't recognize her, and "The Killing," with its grudging empathy for the hated, terrified Custer. In gloating over his death, the protagonist brings about her own.

Big themes, big heart—I was knocked out. I don't know anyone who didn't love Wenona.

"Take me to lunch," the sixth grader dared me—in other words, sneak her off campus, past the basilisk gaze of the principal, Sister Marie Bernadette, and over the mountain pass to Sells, eight miles away. "Naah," she said, tongue protruding, the universal Indian expression of "I'm only kidding." Not yet beautiful—Wenona would become Miss Baboquivari High School—her features jammed small and close together in her round face.

We resumed rehearsing her for a U of A reading.

During the summer I mailed postcards to her and Patrick Lewis-Jose from the Custer battlefield.

By seventh grade she was taller, leaner, greeting me gravely with hand extended, black bangs to her eyes. I was touched to the quick.

Wenona never wrote a timid, trivial, or insincere line. If she had nothing of consequence to say, she produced nothing, and then apologized bitterly, guiltily for it. The poet Jon Anderson invoked "people like myself who want to contend with themselves" when explaining why he wrote. Wenona was one of these, for whatever reason. Along with the lament for her father, Wenona's subject is the struggle with self, over dark temptations in "The Great Spirits," and increasingly with guilt.

I know Wenona was mischievous, insurgent. I know she misbehaved. But what could this lovely person have done that was truly bad? How could she be a pig wallowing in mud? Why didn't she take care of herself, keep herself alive?

When Harty phoned, I exclaimed, with utter conviction, "She's finally with her dad." I don't even believe in such things.

Muriel's marriage to Raymond Ortegas lasted eight years. "He was a good man, a caring man, but he got into drinking," Muriel says. "I knew it wasn't going to work. It was keep my sanity, take care of my children, move on.

"It was very hard for Wenona to deal with. Wenona had seen times when I turned him away, when he was intoxicated. That's the sad part. She was the one closest to him. She wanted her dad to be around. He would share more feelings with her. It was hard trying to explain to her. But she saw a lot of it herself. After a while I think she felt sorry for him. It was like, how can I help my dad? Be nice to him, be kind to him, let him know that I love him."

In a sad irony, Raymond Ortegas was killed by a drunk driver as he walked across a wash, at night. Wenona, fourteen, was called back from a youth conference in California. "She was just devastated," Muriel says. "She went into seclusion. She cried and cried."

It is incredibly generous of Muriel to be talking to me, willing to relive the loss of her children as she attempts to carry on with her life. She now occupies Tanya's home, next door to Wenona's, which is boarded up. The household includes her aged mother, Flora, and her teenaged granddaughter, Georgia—Tanya's daughter.

Muriel is another in the long line of Native women I have known, indefatigably dedicated, who drive themselves sometimes beyond endurance. In thirty years it seems she's worked for every possible tribal social agency, not to mention serving on the ArtsReach Board of Directors, Indian Oasis-Baboquivari School Board, her home Chukud Kuk District Council and the Tohono O'odham Legislative Council, among others. Muriel's father, Thomas Segundo, was a revered figure himself, twice elected Chairman of the tribe.

Even grieving, Wenona excelled in high school. Though the youngest attending, she won the top award at a state competition in student government. She was elected to the Tohono O'odham Youth Council, as vice-chair. Her combative spirit seemed to fuel her ambitions.

As a militant lawyer, she would challenge white supremacy; I passed along bulletins from the Native American Rights Fund.

"Oh, yes, she was active!" Muriel laughs. "Leonard Peltier was her hero." In a controversial trial, Peltier, of the American Indian Movement, was convicted of killing two FBI agents during a shootout at Wounded Knee, South Dakota, in 1975.

Or she would test herself in the Marine Corps. "They told

her, 'We're ready whenever you graduate,'" Muriel says.

Unknown to Muriel, however, Wenona graduated pregnant. "I suspected something because she no longer was talking about school. Two or three weeks after graduation, she told me. Ohh, gosh." Muriel herself, attending the University of Arizona on scholarship, had become pregnant with Tanya after her junior year, and dropped out.

After three years and two daughters, Deshane and Wahela, Wenona married their father, Shane Gregg, a Whiteriver Apache adopted by Anglo missionaries. Tall, good-looking, Shane "seemed well-behaved," Muriel says. "He was a nice person. It wasn't until they got married that the drinking started happening." Shane lost his job, was jailed for repeated DUIs.

"I think Wenona felt like she needed to help him," Muriel says. Soon Wenona was supporting the family financially; temporarily they moved in with Shane's parents.

She was hired by the tribal prosecutor's office as a secretary. Though lacking a degree, she so impressed her bosses that they promoted her to assistant. "It's a lay person, but they were training her. She understood the law, the concepts, how trials were run. Before you know it, she was going to court." It must have seemed like the old—or young—Wenona rising again.

But Wenona herself began drinking, then drugs, marijuana and cocaine.

"I don't know how all this happened," Muriel says. "There were breaks in the marriage, times when her husband was incarcerated, or separations. I think it was too much pressure on her life, and having two little ones to raise. The last two years she gained so much weight—she had just let herself go.

"I was so hurt, seeing her go through that. She lost her job because she was missing days, and got really into her drug addiction. She denied things. 'I'm OK. I don't want you worrying about me.' I worried about the children. People came around to check on them.

"I really sat her down and asked her, 'What are you doing

with your life? I'm going to take the children if you don't go to treatment, if you don't get some help.'

"I got her into detox. She did a lot better when she came out. But this guy…She had this young man that she put so much love and faith in, and really believed that he was going to be good for her and take care of her. For some reason she just could not get over him. She could not get over him.

"Where did I fail her? In life. She was too proud, too ashamed to say what's really bothering her. She felt guilty. And yet she was so strong-willed, you know. She was full of life."

I wonder if Wenona was overcome by sadness. If the weight of her distinguished family was too much to bear for someone so hard on herself, so demanding of herself. If even her own gifts were a burden. But these aren't answers. According to Muriel, Wenona finally had decided to divorce her husband. She had confronted her addiction, completed treatment. There were signs. Her death wasn't inevitable. It happened.

Muriel sets down memorial photo collages, one each for Tanya and Wenona. Tanya, she reminisces, "knew every part of the reservation, because she would be on the back roads looking for rocks, plants, things of nature."

Wenona's gallery includes her senior photo, openly radiant, a hint of teasing in her hooded eyes.

"She was a beautiful child. She was my pride and joy."

During our talk, I've been aware that Muriel's most vivid descriptions of Wenona, by far, are of her horrifying fatal injuries, the damage to her tissue, even the lacerations from the seat belt as it strained and snapped with the impact.

It is cruel that we remember the end so well.

Compared to her agonizing last days and hours, my mother's splendid, courageous lifetime recedes into an impressionistic gauze for me. My father, on the other hand, disappeared from his sailboat, which was found drifting 70 miles off the California coast. For years the lack of finality troubled me, but now I'm grateful to remember him as a living being, not a waterlogged corpse.

Muriel seems to exist in aftermath, parenting one bereaved, teenaged granddaughter, fighting for a relationship with Wenona's two daughters, whose white grandparents threaten to send them away to Ohio. I don't know what bravery, duty and faith sustain her. Clearly she is heartbroken, and not quitting.

Our talk finished, Muriel leads me to the cemetery and then the shrine. "I miss my girls so much," she cries, as we hug by their graves.

On the road north, just before Muriel reaches her turnoff, a yellow school bus pauses at the corner, and a teenaged girl steps out. It is Georgia, Tanya's daughter. Muriel stops to pick her up, and the two proceed up the dirt road, on their new way together.

A couple of weeks after Wenona's death, I held a family writing workshop at the tribal library in Sells. Anticipating Day of the Dead on November 2, I read Wenona's story "The Journey" aloud. The young people were enthralled. They wanted to know who she was, so I told them. If Wenona's writing can inspire others to write also, she is still alive that much.

In response, a high school student, Clarissa Gonzalez, wrote the poem that follows.

# Grandma

She's the early rising sun, the light of
the day,
She's the nightly moon, the light of
the night,
She's the natural plants, the breath
of life,
She's the flowers, the beauty of life,
She's the stars in the sky, the map
of the world,
She's the clouds of rain,
the cleansing shower,
She's the smoke from the sage,
the healing smoke,
She's the food we eat, the wonder of
the world,
She's the strong mountains,
the sense of direction,
She's the babies of the world,
the gift of life,
She's the earth, air, fire, and water,
the elements of life,
longed to see again, until the day
we find the footsteps she left
to get through the path of life.

*—Clarissa Gonzales, 2005*

—*Angela Francisco*

# PATRICK LEWIS-JOSE

Patrick Lewis-Jose is a member of the Akimel O'odham
and Tohono O'odham tribes. Growing up in Nolic, on the Tohono
O'odham Nation, he now lives with his wife and children in her
pueblo of Tesuque, New Mexico.

# The Boy and the Eagle

There was a boy about eighteen years old. He got really mad at his parents because they were going to let him do the plans to a new house, but they went ahead and did their own plans.

Then he ran real fast toward a place he had never been. It was very quiet and had plants of yellow and red, and tall strong trees. When he had found a place to sleep, he slept. The place he slept had a lot of leaves on the ground which had fallen from the tree above.

Overnight he changed into an eagle. When he woke up the next morning, he tried to talk, but his voice was just a loud squawk. Then he looked at himself, and he had feathers on his arms and all over his body. He could see his beak by just looking down. He looked at his feet and could see that his nails were as sharp as a knife.

He went in a little cave that was dark, but not so dark after he built a fire. And after a while he came out and started to fly, but he saw he wasn't very good at it. On his first try he couldn't get off the ground. On his second try he ran off a cliff. He fell to the ground but wasn't hurt. That's when he learned to fly better by flapping his wings a little slower. It took him a while before he started flying so swiftly. The next step he learned was to catch his prey and be cautious in case there was danger. While he was hunting, he heard a rabbit in the bushes, and after a while he could spot it from far away.

Then, about a year later, he saw his family was searching for him, and he also missed them. Then the next day his family went over to a ditch where inside was a small river, and they went in the ditch. They saw a person who was far away, and there, sitting on the river bank, was an eagle which was their son.

As they got closer, he changed, and when he turned around he brushed off his arms. Four feathers fell off his arms, and on his head was a feather. And his hair was very straight as if the wind had been blowing against it.

When they took him home, he found out they had a new addition to their family. It was his brother, a nice little baby who soon will be told of the place his brother will never forget.

And when the boy thought about things, he thought about how fun it was to be an eagle, and how good his vision was, and hearing. But he still had it in his heart, and it was almost like he had two hearts. He goes to visit where he stayed and sometimes turns into an eagle.

*—Patrick Lewis, 4th Grade*

# Fear

Walking on the unfamiliar trail
I felt a dark wind at my back.
Hesitantly I looked back at the black form,
dark, cold, dreadful.
The feeling, like nothing I felt before
The feeling: fear.
The darkness creeping behind you and
as you look back nothing is there.
Running, running,
Running into a dream.
The dream is a cloud, you feel worry free and in
seventh heaven.
Suddenly, darkness. The dream is a nightmare
All around you: Fear,
laughing at you like you have no chance
Fear. Most would crumble and hide. No. You,
Courageously and ever willing to disprove fear
you pick up the sphere of darkness, you
look into the sky where a circle is and beneath
the circle is a web.
With much concentration and a graceful arc
You let the sphere of darkness fly though the circle,
into another dimension.
Gone, gone.

*—Patrick Lewis, 8th Grade*

# The Path

Each grain of sand presented a new pattern
as my feet sank into the soft, moist earth.
Just as my thoughts changed with each new
day.
One foot in front of the other.
This was routine in the way I made my
journey to nowhere.
Nothing mattered I only walked.
My eyes fixated on the ground.
Nothing in particular.
It was me on the path alone with my
thoughts.
I could do nothing but wander.
Wander, as my mind was at constant battle
with my heart. Each taking different paths.
It only ended in confusion.
Who am I?
What am I?
As the frustration began to build I tossed a
stone into the wind. Not knowing or even
caring where it lands.
Who cares, right?
Who cares about anything?
Any soul with an ounce of compassion.
God damn you idiot!
What the hell are you doing?
The voice thundered in my mind, a voice
familiar yet I wondered. Who?
Off in the distance an eagle quietly landed on
a tree stump.
As I drew closer the image shape-shifted and
was more like that of a man.

As was my first instinct I only offered a
shrug.
As shallow as the world had made my mind I
did not understand.
Perhaps, I did not believe.
Maybe my impure thoughts denied me the
access to the spiritual world.
I didn't know.
I only stared as the man stared back.
It was grandfather.
I knew.
His long, dark hair lay back softly.
The expression on his face was solid and it
never changed.
Lines of wisdom were etched on his tired
face.
His mouth rested in what appeared to be a
peaceful frown.
It didn't matter.
I was lost in his eyes.
They were dark and sank deep into his skull.
Like an eagle.
There was more to it.
I looked further.
Beyond anything real.
Inside there was a journey, a story.
One traveled for many years.
The journey brought
strength,
knowledge,
wisdom.
He was intimidating but I stood my ground.
Our minds collaborated as we walked.
His words reflected his knowledge and
wisdom.

He glared into my eyes and seemed to look
inside me and hear my thoughts.
Grandfather said, "Tell me who you are."
The wind whispered to me but I could not
hear though I tried.
I offered no answer. I didn't know.
He spoke softly, "You are your people, your
family.
Remember who you are.
You are the land.
You are the mesquite tree, its roots well into
the earth.
You are the roots of your people.
You gain strength everyday.
Grow.
You are the elements of the earth.
You are the sun, the moon, the stars, the sky.
You are the seed that longs to explode with
life.
Grow.
The river that runs everlasting to the sea.
The sky is my sea.
The world is yours.
You are the hopes and dreams.
Your strength is your heart.
Your heart is the earth.
Follow your heart.
You are the roots of your people.
Grow.
I'll be here.
When the sun awakens over the eastern
horizon.
I'll be here.
When the birds sing sweet songs on a quiet morning.
When the clouds approach and the storm

shouts.
I'll be here.
At night I'll be the stars guiding you.
I'll be here."
"No Grandfather, don't go," I whispered.
Listen to the wind, his voice echoed across
the sunset.
I'll be here.
The words began to drift as he walked away
to the sky.
He walked until his feet no longer touched
the earth.
He was gone.
My thoughts took me back home along the
path.
One foot in front of the other.
A smile once lost had returned as I walked.
Listening, watching.
Looking toward the stars.

—*Patrick Lewis, 10th Grade*

# Summertime

It was summer and
I remember taking long
drinks of Coca Cola that
Grandpa gave me.

Refreshing drinks of
sweet carbonation
and it was good.
Good like redemption

In the sunlight he
looked like he could
have been a great chief.
In the old days.

It was not his preferred
drink
But he shared the good stuff
with me.

We would finish with
that same ahhhh that
sounded like the greatest
sound ever heard.

Down to the ground the shiny
red cans would fall
and the look of satisfaction and
accomplishment shone in our faces.

Beneath our feet the cans
crumbled.

The way we crushed cans
seemed like an art.
inside. crushed. outside. folded.

It was like a ceremonious
dance, our ritual like the
breaking of the
bread.

As the song ended to our carbonation dance
we both looked at each other.
Without saying a word
we knew it was time.

The bags filled and tied
all the memories sealed
and thirst quenched, it was off
to the city...
to trade for more memories.

*—Patrick Lewis-Jose, 12ᵗʰ Grade*

# In the Rain

I can feel it sometimes in the
calm before the storm.
I can feel the rhythm of death
in my feet from the running.

And I can feel the fear in my
stomach as the dust surrounds
me and my feet hurt from
running.

I can hear the bullets fly over-
head like it was the Fourth of
July. And my ears hurt,
from listening.

And I can hear women crying
and the babies.

Bullets are laughing and I can
hear the rhythm of death in the
cries.

I was not there when it all
happened but my eyes
hurt from seeing and my
eyes hurt from crying.

When the rains come I am
blind but I can see it
all like it was only
yesterday.

It's the feeling you get
when you don't know
if you'll remember yesterday,
tomorrow.

And the tears from long ago
times feel fresh from my eyes
as I recall what once
was.

And the songs of the storm
make me remember. Because
you can hear the old songs in
between the shouts of thunder.

The darkness comes close
like an old friend and offers
the only compensation for
years of degradation.

In sleep, dreams come and
dreams go. Sometimes we
forget and sometimes we
remember.

And my head hurts from
dreaming and trying to
remember and trying
to forget.

When the elders speak I can
hear the prayers from
long ago and those prayers
weep for remembrances.

I could see the history of a
people in the elders' eyes but
there are tears in their eyes and
mine
sting from the pain.

Sometimes we forget the way
the song starts or the way
it ends. The song of a
culture.

When the rain sings and
we don't know what it means.
We hear the rhythm of bare feet
dancing and we can't figure it
out.

It's the last drop of a refreshing
drink from the spring of
continuance and all that is left
is but a drop of remembering.

Some say the spring will fill
again from the depths of
Mother Earth.
And we will be full.

Some say the children will
once again bathe in the comfort
of culture and the seeds of heritage
sprout from their hearts.

Some say it will happen again,
that thing called culture and tradition.
The old ones say they can

hear it in the rain.

Maybe, when the bullets stop
flying, when the mothers, the
elders and the babies stop crying,
when we stop running.

If during the rain you can find
the words to the song of life,
the past, and tomorrow.
The song of a people, then
maybe.

I can feel it sometimes in the
calm before the storm.
I can feel the rhythm of a people
in the voices of the children.

In the rain I can hear their new
feet dancing and remembering.
And in my heart the fear of not
knowing is covered with the
hope,

of bare feet gripping the earth
in the rain.

—*Patrick Lewis-Jose, 12ᵗʰ Grade*

◎ ◎ ◎ ◎ ◎ ◎

I've approached each reunion for this book in a state of anxious anticipation. Anxiety in my role as middle-aged, prying white guy. Anticipation toward meeting a former student, for me an impression of memories and printed words on the page, now formed into a grown person.

With Patrick Lewis-Jose there is less suspense. Though I've seen him only rarely since he departed for Stanford University, we've corresponded at intervals. I wrote a recommendation for his admission into Stanford's graduate STEP program. I know the outlines.

Searching for his family home in the desert, squinting for the lone basketball hoop that will mark his turnoff, my eagerness takes a different form, in the question: how did Patrick become Patrick? In Greek mythology, Athena burst full-grown and fully armed from the head of Zeus. That's Patrick. He *always* possessed that gravity and keenness, that unswerving focus. It's as if he wasn't formed but he always *was*.

But of course nobody is that way. So there's the mystery.

Patrick attended fourth grade at Topawa Intermediate, which in 1990 was housed in a Catholic mission school, by agreement with the Indian Oasis-Baboquivari School District, which lacked its own facility. The village of Topawa lies eight miles south of Sells, across a twisting pass through rugged hills thickly forested with saguaro. The road descends into a magnificent vista of desert plain sweeping toward *Waw Giwulk*— Baboquivari Peak—to the east.

According to O'odham tradition, *I'itoi*, Elder Brother, protector of the people, lives in a cave partway up the mountain. The path to *I'itoi*'s cave is a kind of pilgrimage.

The intermediate school, a low-lying complex of red brick, was ruled with an iron hand, but not unkindly, as far as I could tell, by Sister Marie Bernadette, the principal. She at least was gracious to me, and welcomed a creative writing program that could be viewed as (was intended to be?) subversive to conventional order. Order prevailed, in the unadorned brick interiors, rows of desks, structured curriculum, the banning of rock band symbols on clothing or notebooks.

Perhaps Sister had gazed ahead into the abyss—Baboquivari Middle School—and recoiled. Its classrooms could be mini-riots back then. From time to time they still are. Trotsky's perpetual revolution. ArtsReach co-founder Mick Fedullo, the most charismatic, commanding teacher I have known, who has earned immediate devotion in Native classrooms from Arizona to Alaska, was routed from one BMS seventh grade.

My second day in the fourth grade I presented an activity that deals with transformation and its aftereffects. Patrick's response, "The Boy and the Eagle" (first story in portfolio), showed an intuitive understanding of the concept, with real narrative drive. What bowled me over was the ending, "and it was almost like he had two hearts." A small, handsome boy, Patrick had a self-contained air, an almost implacable attentiveness, as if his eyes wanted to suck the marrow of knowledge from one's bones. Gently, of course, politely, respectfully. During revision the following week, I conferenced with him briefly in the teachers' supply room. Instantly he grasped and applied the principles. About a third of the finished version of his story, virtually all the details, was scrawled in the margins of his first draft during those ten minutes.

For example, the opening to the original draft had read:

> There was a man and he got really mad at his parents. Then he ran real fast toward a place he had never been, and when he found a place to sleep, he slept.

It's direct, forceful, but in revision the setting of his transformation is imbued with a natural magic, and the context of the dispute enlarges the character.

"That's Patrick," exclaimed a school aide, when years later I used his story during a family writing workshop. "He lost his power, so he had to get it back."

That Patrick is so formidably self-motivated is fortunate, given the educational climate in which he grew up.

The institution of the public school is alien to Native learning styles—probably to all learning styles, for that matter. It is steeped in Anglo pedagogical theory, history, and culture, taught typically by Anglo teachers, in English. With some exceptions, the intermittent goodwill efforts to respect the language and culture of the students themselves have much the same impact as, say, Black History Month, Holocaust Remembrance Week, or Pancreatic Cancer Awareness Day.

My first year with ArtsReach, I traveled to three campuses in a day, Indian Oasis Primary in Sells, for two extended first grades, Topawa Intermediate for a sixth grade, then back to Sells for high school juniors.

"Extended first" was a euphemism for would-be second-graders who had been retained. They probably were the best writers of that age I've worked with, ever, anywhere, including the most privileged enclaves the public school system has to offer. Their teachers were brilliant, innovative, and consistent in promoting reading and writing. The students created without pause in the morning and revised in the afternoon. "Just don't expect Indian kids to talk up in class," I'd been warned. These kids discussed, they critiqued, they volunteered anecdotes.

The Topawa sixth graders did not, in fact, speak up. I held dialogues with myself at the blackboard. But then they wrote, often quite well.

The juniors said nothing and wrote nothing. By the second day I thought I had failed. Desperate, I began circulating one-to-one with the teenagers, talking them through stories they might write, encouraging them line by line, fishing their crumpled pages out of the trash at the end of class, copying them in the office, and returning them, much to the students' surprise, the next day. Eventually, by the end of two weeks, most had written a story or two. What I learned talking to them was that they had no confidence. Zero. They couldn't believe that any words they committed to paper would be worth anything, so why bother. They were the older brothers and sisters, or cousins or uncles or aunties, of the joyfully prolific, flunked, extended first graders.

What had happened in those intervening years?

Sure, the school system was at fault, and mediocre or terrible teachers, often bigoted teachers. A rez job, living in a remote village or commuting 140 miles a day, with no pay differential, does not always attract the top candidates to the classroom or administrative office. But many were dedicated, capable, even iconoclastic themselves, such as the teacher of those silent sixth graders. The junior English teacher was obviously caring and resourceful. A scattering of O'odham and other Native teachers provided havens, oases, along the journey.

There also seemed to be a gathering apathy as students progressed closer and closer to graduation. Absenteeism approached epidemic proportions by high school. Students openly cursed each other and the teachers, walked in and out of classrooms as they chose. It was as if they looked ahead and their footsteps slowed—toward what? There were no jobs, not even a casino, yet. They were haunted by early deaths of dear ones, family and peers. While they appreciated their wondrous natural environment, virtually no organized recreation was available to them.

There was little to replace what they had been, as a people. This is the dimension too profound for me ever to understand, a legacy of cultural, social, and spiritual destruction partially orchestrated by the occupying powers and partly just the inevitable outcome of occupation.

Often the teenagers' writing erupted through that superficial apathy, with rage and despair.

Increasingly, there would be the encroaching menace of gangs.

In this learning environment Patrick thrived year after year until graduation in 1997. Writing for him was not the escape it can be for many, but simply an extension of his purposefulness, the lightbeam he cut through life.

By then Patrick had grown to over six feet, a star on the varsity basketball team that reached the state finals. He had participated in leadership conferences in Washington, D.C., and at Stanford, to which he'd received a scholarship.

"Culture shock, to say the least," Patrick recalls of his freshman year in Palo Alto. "My father-in-law has a perfect way of describing it, a 'meat-grinder.'

"I remember not being able to sleep the first month there. To be honest, it was light traffic, but it was more than I was used to."

Patrick's home village of Nolic, thirteen miles out of Sells, consists of widely scattered homes, the basketball court, a community hall, and little else. The desert scenery and isolation are spectacular. Patrick, his wife Pinpoquin, twin daughters Camilla and Leanna, and the newborn Emma are visiting his mother Charlene's house, with a small *watto* [ramada] in front and Santa Claus on the roof. Next door lives his Grandpa Charles, in a similar structure of solid block.

"There were definitely moments when I said, wow, this is almost overwhelming," Patrick continues. "Academically, it was a lot more fast-paced. It took extra work to keep up with things."

Did he ever doubt he could make it, I asked.

"I'm too stubborn for that. I didn't give myself a choice."

The "most challenging" episode, he thinks, is when Poquin (his wife's nickname) became pregnant when he was a sophomore. They took two years off for their daughters' infancy, moving to Poquin's pueblo of Tesuque, New Mexico, before resuming and finishing at Stanford, then receiving their Masters degrees in the Stanford Teacher Education Program (STEP). The interruption was "probably a blessing. It helped me come to terms with the fact that things are not always going to be picture-perfect: start, get done in four years. I'd really thought that was the way it was supposed to be."

It had struck me, during Patrick's progress through the Indian Oasis-Baboquivari schools, how little his classmates seemed to resent his drive, studiousness, and success. Perhaps it's because then as now he refused to see himself as special.

"My belief is no!" he declares. "All the people around me are capable. More than capable."

In high school, Patrick had said of ArtsReach, "It amazed me to see my peers becoming very involved in their own writing. I think, 'There's no way that guy is going to have anything worthwhile,' and then he reads his piece and it blows me away. Those students realized that as well, the potential they had. It made me realize that everyone has something great to say in their lives."

In answer to "why me?" Patrick does credit a motivation instilled in him by his grandparents. "As long as I could contribute to making them proud, making them happy, that's what I should be doing. It wasn't so much how to be the best—I just wanted to be the best that I could." Basketball is an example he uses, when he coaches. "I'm the first to admit I wasn't the biggest, fastest, all of that. There were many around me who were more talented than I was, but for whatever reason they didn't push themselves. I tend to believe I outworked them."

But the larger question, to Patrick and his wife, is, "What prevented them? I graduated with forty or so. Every single one of them could have gone to college and made their own choices from there. But that wasn't the reality."

Native students, Patrick and Poquin have decided, require a different kind of education from what they themselves received, and their mission is to help provide it.

"No matter how much our communities bring in the outside world, mainstream society, if that's what you want to call it, no matter how much that gets intertwined in our everyday lives on reservations, in pueblos, in various Indian communities, there are always going to be things that make our experience different," Patrick says.

Negatively, that included the infamous era of coerced boarding school—a kind of mass government kidnapping—for so many Native students. "That stunted our experience. In a historical context, that's very recent history. Up until the middle of the twentieth century, not being able to speak their own language, being taken away and their entire way of thinking being transformed—we're still dealing with that, trying to figure out what it means."

To overturn that legacy, Patrick believes, "The most obvious thing is to incorporate culture. I hear that a lot. But how do we really put that into action?"

His own schooling offered little guidance. "Here we've got this school in the middle of a reservation, there's 99 per cent of the people from our tribe," he recalls. "Yet there's only token emphasis on culture. It's almost nonexistent."

The conflict, as Poquin states it: "How can we focus on culture and still meet science and writing standards?"

She began exploring answers during her first year teaching, at the school she attended herself, a tiny K-6 in Tesuque. One of only two teachers, she handles grades kindergarten through second.

"I learned how to use the knowledge within the community, and realize that it's science," she explains. "Farming is science. Learning about bugs is science. Everything we did turned into a science project, or a science question." For instance, during a tie-dye project, she encouraged her students to form and test hypotheses around color blending. "We had a Native woman to help. We were talking about how we could incorporate traditional dye."

While at Stanford, Poquin discovered a decades-old book concerning pueblo life, *In My Mother's House*, by Ann Nolan Clark. "It was actually poems that kids had written in the classroom. The artwork is by someone in the community. It's the only book that I've ever seen that shows, at the children's level, pueblo dress, pueblo homes, and it shows a picture of our village. You can actually see the house that Patrick and I live in right now. I was thinking if I as a child had been exposed to this, what it might have done for me."

Updating that treasure could promote learning in a culturally relevant way. "The children don't realize that where they live is unique," Poquin says. "Realizing the beauty of the dirt. I plan to get them to put it in a little book, to write things about their community and take pictures with the digital camera, or draw."

During Patrick's initial year teaching, he fought—and won—a different battle. In contrast to Poquin's, his site ten miles down the road, in Pojoaque, is gigantic, with seven classrooms at his third grade level. Of his students, only three were Native, the majority Hispanic.

"Our school district was in the middle of this professional development training, the Baldridge system. It's a really systematic approach to learning, data-driven. The whole school followed it.

"I did very little of it," Patrick says. "I said, to be honest, I'm not comfortable with it. It's intended to have kids become aware of scores, whereas I was more interested in them being aware of what they're actually learning."

So the first-year teacher bucked the principal, the school, the entire district. "I got away with it. I was fortunate that my principal—I was able to gain a lot of respect from her. There was mutual respect there. I was given a lot of freedom."

Central to his teaching philosophy, and methodology, is writing.

"I want to help my students develop a perspective, to think. I was asking them, 'I need to know *your* ideas.' They weren't used to that. They had been exposed to a more technical form of writing. I tried to follow the ArtsReach approach, to have that free and open environment. We did a lot of creative writing. To a certain extent I was successful, to see by the end of the year they were free to express themselves.

"Same thing with the approach to reading. If I'm excited about a book, I can explore it in different ways, and entertain multiple perspectives on things. My own story, people can get different things from it. Part of my upbringing prevents me from feeling, oh, I wrote this so people will feel *this* way. That's really presumptuous."

Patrick read the class his "The Boy and the Eagle"— anonymously. "I never told the class I wrote it. I wanted them to focus on the writing, and I thought it might just get in the way. They actually liked it." He laughs. "A shining moment, if you will, was how we discussed it. They were able to point out different things—"Oh, I liked how the author did this, or how he described this."

I tell "the author" I've taught his story to innumerable classes and workshops, all ages and settings, from the affluent foothills to a group home for incarcerated youth.

Unlike many of my past students, for whom their writing careers are distant episodes, dimly glimpsed, Patrick remembers composing each piece. About "Fear" he says, "Think about that age group, middle school, how that tends to be a notorious time in young people's lives. A lot of times the way we respond to things, the choices that we make, are rooted in fear, and how we decide to deal with that. I guess it was my own way of being able to see it as something tangible that, hey, I can get rid of so I can accomplish things."

While I could view this as yet another example of Patrick's remarkable self-creation, he holds a different answer to my question, and finally I learn what it is. He is the sum of his family.

About his maternal grandparents, Charles and Marcelina Lewis, "I always appreciated how they treated one another, always in a light, respectful manner. Being around the elders was a blessing for me. I got a sense of the way we should be, as a people."

He remains close to his biological father, Kevin Apkaw, an Akimel O'odham (Pima) from the Gila River reservation, between Tucson and Phoenix. "That side of the family has taken me in." Raised by his stepfather, Tony Jose, Patrick says, "I have a great relationship with him. I almost despise the term 'stepfather' because he's so much more than that.

"My Uncle Virgil was the athletic one. I followed his lead athletically."

His Uncle Gary seems to have inspired not only Patrick's writing but the fervent, gritty belief in other human beings that drives him.

"Uncle Gary had a lot of health issues. That made his schooling, the whole social aspect of it, really challenging, especially when he got into high school. The way he dealt with that was through poetry. One of the first things of his I read wasn't the rosiest of poems. It dealt with suicide. I was probably eleven. Although I never experienced those feelings, I did through his writing. The poem was 'Going Where the Lonely Go.'" For a moment Patrick's self-control slips. His voice breaks and halts, and tears fill his eyes. "I was able to see the really difficult issues in his life. They led to alcoholism. He overcame that. He was able to change. Putting that all together made me really proud of him. He started going to Pima College. He finished a year there, and then for financial and health reasons he had to come back. I believe he could have finished. He died in a car crash.

"I always had a tremendous amount of respect for him. I always felt he was capable of so much. I was very impressed by his writings. That helped me continue to express things.

"There is so much good in people. People aren't perfect. Someone makes a mistake, it's easy to judge them as bad people. I have to look at the whole person, the good and the bad. Anything I do, even going into teaching, I wanted to know the good and the bad."

The great good fortune for Patrick and Poquin is that they have each other as partners to share their families, and their ambitious goals.

Eventually, they want to work together, creating "a school with a similar vision. We need to develop ourselves, our understanding of education in general, and how culture and education coexist. The way to develop that knowledge is through teaching."

My fantasy always has been that Patrick will return to the Tohono O'odham Nation and teach there…maybe even with ArtsReach. I tease him with that possibility.

Glancing at Poquin, he laughs heartily. "I'll email you on that one," he says, just loudly enough for her to hear.

"When I was growing up," he says, "the belief was that I'd return and contribute in any way that I can. Now it's expanding more, thinking about Indian communities in general. Where can I be of most use? Not only where I grew up, and where I now live, but to other communities. Education isn't going away. How can we make it ours?"

Patrick accepts, even welcomes the idea that there will be no easy answers, in education or other mysteries. "Even when an elder is telling a story," he says, "they'll end it in a way like, 'That's how *I've* been told.' Never so definitive as to say, that's the answer, that's the word, that's how it is.

"That's the beauty of life in a way. You're always searching for answers. Would you continue the search even if there wasn't going to be that one answer that would explain everything? To me there's beauty in that search."

—*Bernadette Pablo*

# ANTONE FAMILY

Angie and Ernie Antone, both previously married, live in Sells with Angie's daughter Regina Eleando, and grandchildren Maleya Garcia and Charlie Moristo. They are Tohono O'odham. After living with the Antones for a year, Ernie's daughter Deanna Antone moved back to her home in Sacaton, on the Gila River Reservation. She is Tohono O'odham and Akimel O'odham (formerly known as Pima). Erlinda Juan, Angie's eldest daughter, died in an auto accident in 2001.

# Trying To Fly

My dad wanted to go up to the sky so much that he kept trying and trying to learn how to fly. He kept asking people if they could teach him, but people said there was no such thing as flying.

So one day he got tired of asking people. He got a ladder and climbed up on the roof, and tried to jump as hard as he could, but instead he just jumped to the ground. When it was night time he came inside and asked my mom if people could fly. My mom said, "No. People can not fly." When he went to sleep, my father kept saying in his sleep that he wanted to fly.

The next day he went outside and kept trying to fly, but it didn't work. He got so tired of trying that he just quit. Then one day, when we went to sleep I didn't hear him saying anything, so I went into my mom and dad's room, and I didn't see him anywhere. So I went to check if he was outside, but he wasn't. So I went back inside and went to sleep.

Then in the morning he was there. I went to go see him, and I asked him where he was last night. He said that when he was asleep, he went outside, and a man came and told him that it was time to come to spirit land. So he did, and then the man sent him back. My dad said that he flew. I said, "There's no such thing as flying."

But the next day my dad had died. His spirit was with us for four days, and then it went to spirit land and stayed there. Me and my mom were very sad because we missed him a lot.

*—Erlinda Juan, 4ᵗʰ Grade*

# Baboquivari

As day becomes
night I race to
Baboquivari. I
see a rabbit
digging a hole
for his home.
He looks like a
bulldozer.

As I get higher
I hear voices in the wind.
When I get to
the top I
whisper my
deepest secrets
to the setting sun.

*—Regina Johnson-Eleando, 4th Grade*

# The Rain

The rain is so soothing
to my ears. The rain
is like my therapist.
I can tell Rain anything
and the rain won't say
anything.
The rain talks back
but only in soft whispers.
The rain whispers to me
as it hits the ground.
To other people rain is just water
falling from the skies,
but to me it's more
sacred.
Sometimes Rain has to leave me
but I know that it'll return.

*—Regina Johnson-Eleando, 8th Grade*

# Grandmother

Hot, sunny summer afternoon in the desert. My grandmother, Christine, can't wait for the men to finish setting up camp. She and her mother wait patiently on the side and finish up their baskets for the *ba:hidaj*. They are gathering *ba:hidaj* for the wine ceremony.

My grandmother's parents always told her to respect the land, but she never really knew the importance of the land and its plants and animals until today on this hot and sunny afternoon.

While my grandmother was waiting, she decided to explore the campgrounds a little more. Even though she had been going to the same camping grounds for 13 years she never really knew the surroundings. So as she was exploring she was kicking up dust and kicking around rocks. She came upon an ant hill, so she kicked up the dirt and it covered the ant hill. She just kept on walking. Then she heard a little voice say "hey!" She looked back and she looked all around but she didn't see anyone. Then she heard it again. She finally looked down and there was a little ant!

So she got down on her knees and started talking to the ant. The ant said to my grandmother Christine, "Didn't your parents ever teach you to respect your land and all the creatures?"

My grandmother replied, "Yes, well, I never really knew what it meant!"

"Every plant and animal has a meaning!" said the ant.

My grandmother sat on the ground quietly and looked around at her surroundings, and said, "I understand now." She thanked the ant for the great words of wisdom and returned to camp. As the sun set, the saguaro flowers started to bloom.

—*Regina Johnson-Eleando, 8ᵗʰ Grade*

# Heart Rock

She walks through the damp, cold wash.
Home is her destination.
She's searching for motivation
to make it through another day.
The tears stain her beautiful face
her heart broken again.
As she walks kicking up sand
she kicks a rock, looking down at it.
The shape is like a heart.
As she looks closer, there is a little crack
in the middle, but it looks as if somehow
it was mended back together.
This gives her hope that one day
her heart will heal.
She no longer thinks of rocks as nothing.
For even the toughest rocks break down. Sometimes,
eventually, they heal.

*—Regina Johnson-Eleando, 9th Grade*

# Poems

Today I did my work
and waited.
It was as boring as a rose
sitting there, waiting to grow.

I wish I was the wind
so my family and friends
can feel the love and happiness
in my heart.

*—Deanna Antone, 7th Grade*

# The Big Green Umbrella
## (Palo Verde Tree)

The big green umbrella has many branches
and all the different colors, green, brown
yellow and black.
Green like lettuce when it's freshly picked
 (I love lettuce).
Brown like us Tohono O'odham people.
Yellow like the shining sun.
Black like the color of my youngest daughter's
long hair.
And with the red ants, that all have their places to go,
in their own little world.

*—Angie Antone, 2003*

# Cloud Bed and the Rainbow

One cool and cloudy evening, we went to a dance where Gina's uncle was playing. The music was really loud, because it was in a village where only a few people lived.

Gina's uncle Kel hit the cymbals on his drums, so hard that the vibration shot straight up, to all those clouds in the sky. Then it started raining, and before you knew it, there was a giant rainbow of many colors. So we walked up to the rainbow to get to the clouds.

Then we finally got to lie on a very soft bed, without springs sticking out.

*—Angie Antone, 2004*

# Security Officer

Let me tell you a story about these brave men of
Sells Hospital Security.

Security is their job, enforcing government rules,
regulations, and policies, and they do their job well. They
don't complain, nor do they ask for rewards, just doing
their job.

The job that they face each day or night is
protecting and serving the people and the many clients
that enter the hospital, protecting those who care
for others and the property of Sells Hospital and its
residents from harm's way, and detaining perpetrators.

These brave men work many hours and a lot of
overtime and hardly spend time with their family and
kids at home. Needing a rest to start a new shift, only
to have his family understand why he must go to work
on his day off or work overtime. He hugs and kisses the
children and wife good night, or "see you later" words.
Neglecting his own life and those of his family to *protect
and serve.*

These brave men work 24 hours 7 days a week,
day or night and in unstable weather conditions, sunny,
snowing, raining, hot or cold. They don't complain as
long as they're out doing their job *protecting and serving.*

Many times these men are put to the test and
put in many situations, but given negative feedback
because of 1 or 2 mistakes, and we all look bad. These
are the men that will take it no matter what the cause.
It's part of the job. But what people don't know is these
men have feelings, too. Some hide them, some cry
inside, some have nightmares, and some take it away
because someone has to. Some feel angry because no
one understands and feel neglected because he thinks

back to the cold days and nights that he was the one out protecting while people were inside their homes or hiding from the rain, cold, or the hot sun while he's outside doing his job. No handshake or a "job well done" as long as he is out doing his job, and that is protect and serve.

These are the brave men of Sells Hospital Security Officers.

*—Security #2, Ernie Antone, 2003*

◎　◎　◎　◎　◎　◎

On August 30, 2001, Angie Antone's family suffered
lasting trauma when Angie's oldest daughter, Erlinda Juan, missed
a turn and died in an auto crash. She had been drinking. Her
toddler daughter, Maleya, was grievously injured. Erlinda was
nineteen.

Erlinda had published two pieces in *Dancing with the
Wind*. Her story "Trying To Fly" was among the most haunting I
had read. The figure of the father was so poignant and complex, a
man who yearns, even foolishly, to fly, and finally does so, only in
death. I always wondered how a fourth grader had written it.

I met Erlinda again, shortly before the fatal accident,
but I didn't know it. She attended one of my first family writing
workshops along with her sister, Regina Johnson-Eleando,
and their mother. Angie had been assigned the workshop as a
family liaison for the school district. Regina (Gina) I recognized
as an ArtsReach author. But as Angie recalls, "Er didn't write
anything then," and so I don't remember her. I didn't know that
Erlinda Juan was Angie Antone's daughter. Only after Angie and
Gina began writing about their lost loved one did I make the
connection.

Angie and Gina were among my most faithful writers,
attending numerous workshops even when Angie's job didn't
require it. I believe strongly in family writing, in the home as
a center of education. When parents and children, aunties and
uncles, *tatas* and *nanas*, siblings and cousins, write together, they
are both support and audience for each other, both of which
writers need.

Angie and her family were a realization of that vision.
When I began a writing group in Sells, the nucleus was Angie
and Gina, Maleya (drawing pictures and forming letters), Angie's

husband Ernie, and his daughter Deanna.

A vision is not an ideal. The professional writer clings to discipline, hunkering down daily at the computer, regardless of health, mood, or inclination, *producing*, dammit. The reality of the Antone family was more like this: "Kit's class is in 45 minutes. Man, I've got to write something!"

But write they did, and shared it. Gina read at the University of Arizona and the Amerind Foundation. Angie, Ernie, and Deanna read at the Tohono O'odham Nation Legislative Council Chambers, in Sells.

"It brought out stuff that was inside my head," Angie reflects, during a family interview in October of 2008. "When you put it on paper, and you read it, it clears your mind. I wrote something, and it's going out somewhere, to somebody."

"I've always liked to write," Gina says. "I'm not really open with my emotions. Writing is a way to express them."

Ernie decides that he writes often "out of anger." The piece he read publicly, "Security Officer," emerged because "people don't know how we feel. In the law enforcement field, when you catch somebody doing something, they hate you. We're the peacekeepers, but they don't see it that way. Times like that, when I'm upset, at work when the night is quiet, I type things out on the computer. But then I end up deleting everything."

"Security Officer," the exception, survived perhaps because it fulfilled his assignment for the writing group. Ernie works graveyard for the Indian Health Service hospital in Sells.

I bragged about this writing family, the Antones, among friends and colleagues, in presentations to national and state conferences. It's reassuring, then, heartening, on this unseasonably warm October morning, to find them gathered around a card table, under a *watto*, surrounded by desert brush at their rented home on the outskirts of Sells—Angie, Ernie, Gina, Maleya, looking for all the world like a family writing workshop waiting to happen.

It's a relaxed, often comical conversation, considering the

directions it takes—life and death, the tangle of family, drinking.
As it happens, the weight of the past lies palpably on
this gathering. Days earlier, Angie had driven Maleya to Tucson
Medical Center, concerning an upcoming surgery for her
foot. Maleya's physical and cognitive injuries remain severe. I
remember her limping heavily in a leg brace. Now she appears
outwardly whole, her long, black hair combed back simply, eyes
inquisitive. During the entire interview her fingers intertwine
with Gina's. "There are still a lot of medical issues inside her body,"
Angie says.

Meanwhile, this very afternoon Regina Johnson-Eleando
will initiate proceedings in tribal court, to rename herself as
simply Regina Eleando. Once again Gina asserts her identity amid
the bewildering array of kinships that adults have created for her.

Even as a fourth grader, Gina had struck me as a person
firmly planted in a sense of self. In its thoughtfulness and dignity,
her writing reinforces the impression. She still exudes that quality,
more exotic-looking now with her black Egyptian-esque eyeliner
and lip ring. But it's been hard-won. "My dad, my sister's dad, all
of it, it's been crazy."

"Johnson" is Gina's biological father, the name taken from
the stepfather who raised him. When Gina was three, Norman
Johnson added "Eleando"—his biological father—to Gina's and
his name, and to her sister Micaela's, a daughter from a previous
relationship.

"All through school I didn't like it, because my name
would never fit anywhere," Gina laughs.

Erlinda had a different father from Gina's and Micaela's.
Recently, Angie has unofficially adopted Charlie, a grandson from
her other daughter, Alana Gomez; Alana's own father, different
from Erlinda's or Gina's, recently died.

Apparently Gina's dad found the double name
cumbersome, too, because he's dropped the "Eleando" and
reverted to "Johnson."

"So," I say, trying to summarize, "They're all Johnsons

202    Here I Am a Writer

again and you're going to be an Eleando."

"Yeah! No disrespect to my dad's stepdad," Gina says, "but I never knew him, and I grew up knowing my grandpa that carries Eleando."

The family ties have unsnarled considerably, though, since Angie and Ernie married, eleven years ago.

"This family sitting here is the most stability I've ever had," Gina says. "I'm really thankful. Ernie's been the one who supported me and raised me since I was seven."

In all innocence, I inquire how Angie and Ernie met. The assembly collapses into laughter.

"You can tell him." Angie nods to Ernie.

"Which version do you want?" Gina says.

The gist is this: Angie was hospitalized at Indian Health Service, temporarily in a wheelchair, and Ernie, then working the day shift, volunteered to push her to ER.

"In ER, I helped her onto the gurney," Ernie says. "I said, 'All right, I'll see you.'

"She said, 'Thank you.'" Ernie imitates an exaggerated, quavering voice.

"The next night, we shift-changed to evening. I was walking down the ward, and I just happened to look in the room where she was at. 'Hey, what are you doing here?' I had my hands on the rail, and she was like 'Thank you for bringing me in there.' She put a tight squeeze on my pinkie, and I'm like, whoa!

"'Tha-a-ank you-u-u,' she said.

"I said, 'Rest and take care of yourself.'

"After that, when she got discharged from the hospital, I started receiving calls. I was even at a family wake, and she came over with a plate of food. Wow!"

Angie, her face usually so impassive under iron-gray curls, giggles.

Years later, eating breakfast with members of his band, Native Thunder *Mumsigo*, Ernie told them the story. "You're the love doctor, huh?" they said.

Long ago, during an adult writing workshop at Northland Pioneer College, I introduced a quirky exercise in which one writer creates a character sketch, and a partner writes a story for that character. In response to my partner, I wrote about a house uprooted by a flood and carried out to sea. Intuitive currents were passing through the group that night, and it emerged that my partner's character had been an alcoholic, though the sketch hadn't mentioned so. My story, she said, was a metaphor for her family life.

Angie's mother is an alcoholic. When Angie's only sister died in July '08, "the hardest part—and I was trying to be strong—was that my mother wasn't there. She wasn't there at the wake or the funeral," Angie says. "Alcohol played a role in her life at that time."

According to Gina, Norman Johnson is an alcoholic, too. "Dad is recovering, or whatever. He certainly did stop at some point and did try to raise me. But he told me flat out he couldn't handle me."

Just over two years ago, Gina tried living with him. "Actually, these guys sent me away," she says to boisterous laughter. "I guess that was my difficult…I was taking off, sneaking out."

"The teenage years," Ernie finishes.

"During the time my dad was in prison," Gina says, "it was, like, 'I'm going to make life better for you,' and all these promises. He started drinking again, it went out the window."

Angie herself was a drinker, until quitting cold eight years ago, a mutual pact with Ernie.

Before then, "When these guys were drinking, Erlinda would always be the one there for me. In a lot of ways, she took care of me," Gina says. "She's my only sister I ever had any real connection with."

Until Erlinda herself fell victim to alcohol.

Over the years Gina's and Angie's writing has gnawed at the pain of Erlinda's death. Playing volleyball was "carrying the memory of my sister with me," for Gina. "I remember always wanting to be like her." Gina's poem "Heart Rock" dangles the possibility of mending, but as she says now, "It was hard. It still is. I'm glad Maleya's here. She acts like Erlinda so much."

Thumbing through Angie's collected papers, I read, "I have gone through grief, losing my 19 yr. old daughter...referring to my late daughter—Erlinda May Rose Juan...As I sit, for that one moment, in silence, I wonder about my oldest daughter, who is now with the Lord. She is missed so much by everyone."

Surprisingly to some, the agonizing loss didn't shake Angie's sobriety—quite the opposite. "An aunt of mine, my uncle's wife, told me that she thought I would fall off the wagon. It didn't come close to that. I got stronger, knowing that I had to take care of Maleya along with Gina, with the help of Ernie."

"I'm thankful that she's sober and taking care of us, and the grandkids," Ernie says. Especially because he's chosen a different course. "Well, she's sober. I'm not. I can't hide it," he says.

"I guess it was Ernie's choice to drink again," Angie says. "The thing about it was, he stays home and drinks. Friends try to tell him, 'Let's go here' or 'Let's go there.' He doesn't like to go anywhere. Or if he tries to go somewhere with them, he wants to come back right away."

Yes, but—

The past weekend, after Native Thunder's gig in the town of Maricopa, Ernie stayed out all night. "It was upsetting," Angie admits. "We'd borrowed a friend's vehicle, and he had it. He doesn't drive when he drinks. But this time, I don't know what happened."

It's a discordant note in this ongoing tale of resilience and recovery.

Only a month before, the family moved from a rental complex into their solid, whitewashed stucco home. Supported by her husband and daughter, Angie has her Associate's degree in sight, from Tohono O'odham Community College. Her program guarantees her a job. Her preference would be the Tohono

O'odham Police Department, for whom she cooked off and on over several years. Now she would seek an administrative assistant position.

"I can't get used to it, going to school and being here, doing homework," Angie says. "I've always worked. I keep wanting to say I'm going to quit and find a job. These two keep saying, 'You're almost there.'"

"I always tell her, 'Keep going.' We can live on what I make, or what we have, rather," Ernie says.

"Then he jokes and says he's going to retire!"

Ernie laughs heartily. "You get your fifty-dollar-an-hour job and I'm going to kick back."

It's the banter of a close-knit couple.

Gina, too, is nearing her goal of graduating from high school, one semester late. She's also become a godmother to her best friend's daughter, Nevaeh, a name Gina chose. "It's 'heaven' backwards. She has a big impact on my life. In a way I feel as if she's my daughter. I've grown up a lot. I realize I'm getting older, and these guys need help with the bills."

Gina has had a taste of life outside her accustomed family. "I stayed with my dad for maybe two months. I would get really homesick. I'd get to the point where I'd just cry. I asked my mom, come pick me up! She brought me back home."

Her stepsister Deanna, Ernie's daughter, felt similarly lonely during her year with the Antones, when she was part of the writing group. "She was trying to make a connection," Angie believes. After returning to her mother, Deanna graduated high school a year early. "She's doing OK," Angie says.

The sturdy house, hardworking dad, the women on track toward their education and a better life. It's hard to hear floodwaters rising in this happy scene. But last weekend, "I don't know what made Ernie go out after they got back," Angie says. "I was worried."

The shadow of the past is impossible to banish. "When that happened with Erlinda," Angie says, "when Gina was going someplace, I was saying, 'Call me when you get there.' I was calling Ernie constantly at work. It was a phase I was going through. 'Call me.' I think Gina got tired of me saying that."

No argument there. "I think that explains the whole taking-off thing," Gina laughs.

Gina's own attitude toward alcohol? "I've known the effects, in a big way, because of the people who drank around me. I don't think I'd let myself get to the point where I throw it all away because of drinking."

The flood could be miles away now, receding harmlessly into the sands of a desert wash. Or it might be lapping at those white stucco walls.

Of course they write. They're the Antones, aren't they? And Johnson-Eleando. Minus Johnson. Almost.

Given all the troubles endured, induced, contained, surmounted and not, I suggest they would bring some serious chops to a problem story [see p. 228].

Their writing allows me to jot notes of my own and sink into the surroundings, the gentle heat, insects' buzz, the astounding variety and calls of the fluttering birds. A breeze rattles the *watto*'s metal roof—traditional in function if not in materials. Its shade not only cools us but surrounds us and thereby connects us. For these moments we are that dream of mine, a writing community. These are great people, I'm thinking, all the more compelling for their flaws as well as their strengths. Ernie is someone with whom I'd enjoy sitting down to a couple of beers. Now there's an insane idea. Let me do my part to breach the levee and sneak the waters in. The anathema of the reporter—becoming the story himself.

The concept for this project, begun two years ago, was as neat and clean as a blank sheet of paper. Imprint my students upon it, their old writings, their life stories, their new writings. But obviously, in so doing I've left the heavy mark of my own hand. My subjectivity guided my questions, my interpretations of the responses. I've crept into the spaces between their words, waving at you folks out there.

How much have I altered my subject by studying it, the observer effect? In most cases, I suspect, not much. No more than the desert breeze will guide the words those hands are composing around me, under the *watto*.

But I can hope that renewed attention to her works will rekindle Josie Frye's aspirations as a writer. Already she's agreed to assist me in an upcoming series of family writing workshops on the rez. Could she take over this work some day?

And I can terrify myself by wondering how the publication of this book, should it occur, might provoke Martín Acuña further against Marisa Yucupicio. Or could it even protect her, Martín's awareness that he is acting on a larger stage? Or will it subside into complete irrelevance after his ten years in prison?

Here at Writing Club Redux, the responses could not be more diverse. (See the set that follows.) Angie has distilled the essence of our conversation. Gina has introduced an entirely new biographical note, a boyfriend. Maleya, soliciting spelling help from Gina and Angie, has written what she loves.

Ernie raises the stakes on himself. "The O'odham *pa-yahsa*—that's me," he readily confesses. Clown, from the Spanish *payaso*. "When I'm drunk, I do many crazy things, or say many crazy words.

"I try really hard. I'm thankful that these guys put up with me, regardless of what I said right here about getting mad and doing crazy things, they put up with me. Sometimes they just don't bother with me."

"Ignore it," Angie says.

"They obviously love you, too," I say.

Ernie laughs. "If that's how they feel about it. I'm not going to force them to, you know. They take care of me, but sometimes, like Angie, she gets tired of it. I just leave 'em alone."

At the same time, Angie says, "The kids all call Ernie

Grandpa. We call him Grandpa, too. Gina's goddaughter calls him Grandpa, too. He's Grandpa to all of us. He's not Ernie. I call him Grandpa, too."

"When Angie was explaining about last weekend"—here Ernie addresses the aftermath of the Maricopa trip—"when I drink a beer, I worry about my safety, I worry about others' safety. Even when I had my old car, she would take the keys away from me. Or I'll give them to her voluntarily. The other part has to do with fellow officers, in that we're all part of law enforcement. I know all the officers here. I know some of the guys out at Customs, Rangers, Corrections. I don't want to mess up that relationship, because I work with them. As much as I think that way, as much as I do it that way, still, like somebody told me, 'One of these days you're going to end up doing something. You're going to take the wrong step. You're going to be in handcuffs.'"

Ernie's career with IHS spans fifteen-and-a-half years, thirteen in security.

"I'm not going to lie," he says. "I even tell the officers when I run into them. They don't drink like me. I just come straight out and say, 'I got my beer.' I drink at home, where I'm safe, not walking around either getting beat up by these gangsters or whomever, or getting shot at. Angie comes out and checks on us if I have my friends over, playing our instruments. At least there are people who care enough about us—even like Angie, she sits with us, or like Gina, she'll be hanging around with us because she likes music." Native Thunder *Mumsigo* plays chicken scratch, also known as *waila*.

The *chukud pa-yahsa* in Ernie's story is an owl, often, in O'odham belief, the spirit of someone who has passed on. Most O'odham I've spoken to consider them ominous, but some describe them as messengers or even protectors.

To me, Ernie's *chukud pa-yahsa* is unsettlingly ambiguous. Is he Ernie's companion or pursuer? If the O'odham *pa-yahsa* is "gone, went away, and never been seen or heard again," is it the drinker who no longer exists, exorcised from Ernie's character, or is it Ernie himself, done for?

"Whenever that light hits me, to say, hey, you've got to quit drinking, wanting to be that clown, maybe that's the time I'll quit. I wrote about him running away...he's gone. Everything's gone. The way I act when I'm drinking, when I sober up that part's going to be gone."

"So the owl is taking care of you?" Though a lover of ambiguity, I'm anxiously trying to pin the author down. But he won't oblige.

Ernie laughs enigmatically. "Laughing at me."

Ambiguity is the delight of literature. As readers, we savor the zest of an essential truth, that there is no absolute knowledge, no certainty. In real life, it causes us to close our eyes, hold our breath, and hope.

# Untitled

My cats play with me. Sweetie and Rainbow. I like to play with Sweetie. I love Rainbow. Charlie is my cousin because I take care of him. I love you Charlie.

—*Maleya Garcia, 2008*

# October Waiting

It's mid-October and
she sits waiting...
It's been a 20-month wait
and still going.
He's there
she's here
with more than a few states between them.
She loves him, he loves her.
There's no doubt about it
even though it's been questioned by many.
They've faced many obstacles
this one being the biggest.
Commitment and trust is what makes
their love strong enough to face any terrain.
She's still here
he's still there
with more than a few states between them.
He still loves her. She still loves him.
It's mid-October and
she's still waiting...
knowing he'll return.

—*Regina Eleando, 2008*

212 Here I Am a Writer

# My Family Is "My Family"

My family is my family, and I thank our Creator for our lives. Having to lose my oldest daughter, then gaining her daughter, has brought joy into my family. And then learning to take care of my now handicapped granddaughter. Scared but willing to, with open arms. Taking care of my other family as well, and working at the same time. And staying on the wagon, staying away from alcohol. Taking it one day at a time. And now it has been eight years. The years went by so fast because as a family we went through hardships, pain, grief, and happiness. And as a family we have learned or are still learning to cope with these things that come into our lives. And then having to lose my only sister. My family and I were very close to her. That made me a stronger person, knowing that you never know when things can happen, whether it may be sadness or happiness. And then having my second daughter lose her dad, and bringing us closer. Since I never really knew her. I'm getting to know her day by day, as well as my other family members getting to know her. She has two boys, age 7 and 1. So now I have 3 wonderful grandchildren. And I love my family, because they are my family.

*—Angie Antone, 2008*

# O'odham *Pa-yahsa*

When I'm drunk I do so many crazy things or say many crazy words. Being that O'odham *pa-yahsa*, just making people laugh with all my crazy acts. Yet they only laugh at me because I'm drunk. The O'odham *pa-yahsa* becomes a mad *pa-yahsa*, getting angry, hurting other people physically and emotionally and leaving them with scars for the rest of their lives.

One day this O'odham *pa-yahsa* was walking along a dusty road when he was met by a *chukud pa-yahsa* [owl clown]. He was making fun of the O'odham *pa-yahsa* because he was drunk and crying, not wanting to be the *pa-yahsa* because he was hurting too many people. So the O'odham *pa-yahsa* ran away, and still the *chukud pa-yahsa* followed him. The O'odham *pa-yahsa* is gone, gone, went away, and never has been seen or heard again.

—*Ernie Antone, 2008*

# You Are the Writing Teacher

Anyone can teach creative writing to kids. There, I'm out of a job. Or maybe not, since much of my profession relies on that confidence.

Teacher evaluations of my residencies have tended to describe my style as "low-key," approvingly, as in "nonthreatening," "unintimidating," "gentle," or "calm." Initially I was somewhat deflated at this. Gee, I thought I was pretty dynamic.

The point is, you don't have to be—what? Elvis? Madonna? Richard Simmons? Batman? I'm betraying my age here—to make this work. Just believe in it. I do. What power I have as a teacher stems from the absolute conviction that what I'm doing is important, and that the students can, and will, succeed at it.

While ArtsReach instructors such as Mick Fedullo and Diné (Navajo) poet Sherwin Bitsui can inspire out-and-out fervor among their students, my kids write awfully well, too.

This concluding section is a brief how-to manual, for those who teach—or would like to teach—creative writing to their own students or children. It touches upon methodologies and samples some of the writing activities that helped generate stories and poems featured in this book. Of course, these materials represent my approach only, one among innumerable others. But it's a start.

You may have to overcome an innate skepticism. Only real writers can teach this kind of thing, right? And maybe you don't even *like* writing.

Initially, many of the teachers I've trained were incredulous at the idea. Not to mention reluctant. But when they conscientiously studied the model activities, delivering them with relaxed authority, they succeeded. Their students wrote stories and poems. The teachers' relief and delight at this still gratify me. Some teachers presented the material better than I did, with their own personal wrinkles, or modifications that I've borrowed myself. Many invented their own activities.

To be honest, when the teachers didn't prepare, and read the directions haltingly and woodenly, they flopped.

Family writing workshops exist to promote writing in the home. The Antone family, and others, are the proof of this principle.

So, in other words, this teaching course is for you. Whoever you might be. You can do this.

Before we go on, some may ask ourselves, *Should* we do this? In the case of Native students, non-Native teachers such as I may feel uncomfortably complicit as colonists. After all, aren't we guided by our mainstream American, or Western European-derived—call it what you will—standards and aesthetics? Aren't we contributing insidiously to assimilation even as we try to help students find their authentic voice?

For instance, the transcriptions of Native oral stories often lack the formal resolution of a short story from the Western canon. But this isn't surprising if each narrative is only a strand of the larger story, the all-surrounding web or maze. Such a decisive ending would be artificial. Similarly, oral, recited literature achieves an incantatory quality that an academic critic might label repetitious.

The late Josiah Moore, twice Chairman of the Tohono O'odham Nation and briefly my colleague at the Arizona Department of Education, guided me in this as in other ways.

A devout believer in education, he convinced me that, in today's reality, the value of writing for ArtsReach's students overrode any of the cultural hazards I might raise.

"Trust your students," he reassured me. "They'll take what they need from you and, the rest..." The implication was obvious.

The "rest" will go on the trash heap.

I fretted that in using traditional stories to teach I might be trespassing in some way. "If they were secret, you wouldn't know them," Josiah said.

I have come to believe the students do carry an ingrained sensitivity, a vigilance, that will protect them from clumsiness on my part. I remember one example most fondly. Introducing a tale to third graders, I said, "I'm going to tell you a legend..."

"No! No! You can't do that now!" several interrupted me. It was not the winter storytelling season.

"...from Africa," I finished.

"Ohh." Everyone sat back, relieved, in their chairs. I was moved, heartened, to see them rally protectively around their beliefs, and also, it seemed, around me, so that I wouldn't do wrong.

I think I'm right to worry, but not go overboard with it. After all, who am I but just a guy who traipses into their schools and minds for a week or two, while they have their centuries-old culture, their extended families, the wealth of their daily experiences arrayed against any damage I might do.

Most classroom teachers, aware of their year-long impact, have the good heart and good sense to respect and study their students' backgrounds and belief systems. At the very least, we can avoid the worst blunders, such as telling a story out of season. But more, we can expand that appreciation by introducing Native models, professionals and students, into our writing instruction.

I don't presume to recommend a list of Native authors, though those cited in this book would be a good starting point. Search the net, sample a few in the library, and buy those who excite you. Your honest enthusiasm will help sway your students. The young ArtsReach authors featured here are a marvelous resource. If you want more, contact ArtsReach for copies of the annual anthology, *Dancing with the Wind*:

ArtsReach Writing Programs
Tucson Indian Center
97 E. Congress St., Suite 101
Tucson, AZ 85702

I'm not a theorist by nature. I'm in favor of what works.
Roaming the halls with a bullhorn and baseball bat might not
be my style, but apparently it worked for the principal portrayed
in the movie *Lean on Me*. I've witnessed a high school teacher
allowing himself to be picked up by the heels and dangled by a
student. *Anarchy*, I quaked to myself. But the student loved that
teacher. The act, believe it or not, was a measure of trust.

So the philosophy here is pragmatic, based on years of
empirical results, successes and failures.

Some academicians, I've found, approach the public
school arena as if it were an MFA program, composed of eager
students receptive to every nuance of the literary art. They pitch
their instructional theories accordingly.

But in fact these students are conscripts. They didn't ask
to be in school in the first place, and many would rather not be,
much less writing. Their attitude toward writing could be summed
up by Ande Escalante's "agggh."

At least this is true of many of my students, and if you're a
teacher, maybe yours, too.

Writing must be made to invite them, excite them,
encourage them, and enable them to succeed. If they fail, we, the
teachers, failed.

Some students are second language learners. Some have
been labeled "below grade level" or "falls far below the standard."
They already may view writing as another badge of inadequacy.
The accomplished writers have their own anxieties, that they may
not perform as well as they're supposed to. They flinch at the red
pencil, like little welts and cuts on their compositions.

We have to break through all that.

**Here's my first fundamental principle: We must attract our potential writers.**

One way is to begin telling or reading stories and poems that appeal to them, with themes that are easy to apply.

The worst classroom in which I've taught was a fourth grade. The teacher had given up, utterly. Students chatted, shouted, and played as if she weren't there. Fights broke out. A boy hopped onto her desk and walked across it, narrowly avoiding her inert hand. She did nothing. But when I began telling about a showoff who lost his eyeballs, the classroom stilled. It was nearly miraculous. Of course, when the story ended and it was time to write, the uproar resumed. Still, though, most of the students attempted their own stories, concentrating through the din.

With younger students, particularly, I may use a collective classroom story as a model. For instance, in presenting the "Problem Story," I often enlist the class in creating one on the spot.

*What problem is our story about?* I might ask.

"A coyote has a broken leg," someone volunteers.

*Why is that problem important?*

"He can't run."

"He can't play."

"He can't catch food."

*If he can't catch food, why is that important?*

"He'll starve to death."

*Let's not kill off our character. What could happen before that?*

"He'll get really hungry."

*How would we know that?*

"He's skinny."

"He's scraggly."

"His ribs stick out."

"He's eating rabbit poop."

And so on, through all the phases of the story.

Instructors may use a different stimulus, such as a photo, painting, a brief skit, a game. But the intent is the same: Attract.

Stimulate, so that the discussion itself is a form of pre-writing. My favorite indication of this was the student who asked, in his politest tone, "Could you be quiet so we can start writing now?"

**Second principle: Balance guidance and freedom. Give the students a process, a focus, while opening up content as much as possible.**

If I taught creative writing consistently to a class for an entire year, eventually I'd be able to say, "Today we're writing a story," sit back in the chair, plug in my iPod, and watch birds fly by the window. But neither a brief residency, nor the demands of most teachers' test-driven curricula, permit that.

Remember, the majority of our student writers are not volunteers. They have not arrived with their writing gear packed in their heads. Instead, they've been dropped in the midst of a trackless desert. Telling them, "write a story" is like saying, "find Moose Jaw, Saskatchewan." They appreciate a map. They can deviate from that map, or throw it away, but at least they have something to go on.

Most of my writing activities, then, occur in stages. Sometimes I present all stages at the outset, sometimes dole them out one by one as students write.

Thus "The Girl Who Turned into a Horse" [p. 237] asks writers to consider three stages of the story: how a person was turned into something else, what it was like to be that thing, and how, after resuming human form, she was different from her old self. There's a process to grab onto, but how the writers fill it is up to them. In fact, if students ask, "Can an animal turn into a person instead?" I say yes. If they say, "What if the armadillo doesn't turn back into a person?" I answer, "Fine, then your ending is to figure out why he doesn't." Any option they raise, I say yes. If they want to write something else altogether, I say yes. My directions actually are suggestions.

In writing a persuasion, say, or comparison-contrast paper, students must follow directions. I'm teaching particular

220 Here I Am a Writer

rhetorical skills, and if students don't perform them, they won't learn them.

But creative writing is different. The aim is not to follow rules but to make something that never existed before. However the student gets there is fine with me.

Meanwhile, by concentrating on one part of a story at a time, our apprentice writers typically produce drafts that are longer and better developed than they're used to, setting a new standard for themselves.

**Third principle: Try to anticipate your students' response to the writing activity.**

If possible, do the activity yourself. Write the story or poem.

If not, at least imagine your students receiving those directions. What might not be clear? What could require specific examples? How can you broaden the scope of what's possible in their stories or poems? What snippets of personal commentary or anecdote would dramatize your presentation? How can you head off potential problems or blind alleys? How can you make the activity work for everyone?

Most importantly, what do you want your students to gain from this writing? With "The Girl Who Turned into a Horse," for example, I long for them to take that leap, to imagine another state of being, and I'm determined that they will use the skill of sensory detail to do so. I want them to probe what transformation means to their characters, and by extension, to all of us. When I understand my goals, and allow myself to be fascinated by them, my enthusiasm is contagious.

**Fourth principle: Provide that natural reward of the writing process, an audience.**

I read student stories and poems back to the class, anonymously, if the authors so choose. (In rare cases, if the material seems too personal or volatile, I'll consult with the writer about not sharing the piece at all. Writings that violate classroom norms of taste or subject matter won't be read aloud. If students fall into a rut, lots of fart stories, say, or dancing unicorn poems, I'll declare a moratorium on reading those.)

For the author and the audience, this public hearing is an incentive to write better…or at all. More than one difficult residency has turned around when students were exposed to the expression of their peers. "Oh, yeah, that's pretty cool. I can do that."

If you have time, encourage the students to present their own work.

Reading orally is like informal publication. You can go a step further by displaying writings, or actually publishing them, even if only by entering them on computer and binding them together. My classroom teacher associates have produced books, either by hand or through school or district printing facilities. Students enjoy making and illustrating their own books.

**Fifth principle: Revision is how writers get better.**

A first draft is for the writer, the emotional release, the pulse of creation. But subsequent drafts are for the reader. Writers refine and rethink their material based on the desired effect on the reader. This is a far more inclusive and inviting dictum than "Fix it."

Revision is positive. It's making your story or poem better—no matter how good it may be in the first place—and thus more memorable for the reader.

Teachers tell me their classes balk at revision. It does require effort to overcome the aura of stigma: my story is broken and must be fixed, and I have to rewrite it and my hand will get tired.

I begin with my traveling exhibit, a worn backpack stuffed with weathered folders holding smudged rags of manuscript. This constitutes all the drafts of an early story that became widely anthologized, scribbled scraps, a notebook and typed pages overrun with margin notes, cross-outs, insertions—the revision process laid bare in the precomputer era. Then I show the story in the bland, pristine authority of its published state.

The bad news is that stories are not perfectible, I tell the class, not like your times tables or a mathematical proof. They can only get better and better. You're revising not because you're students but because you're writers, and that's what writers do.

I choose a couple of class stories to workshop aloud— the most popular ones. See? Even these can be made better. We entertain suggestions from the students, and my own. Often the author joins in.

In thirty years, I've never had a class resist revision, from first grade on up. Most come to embrace it wholeheartedly. Individual students? Some have cried. More have argued. But when we revise even one line together, almost all are won over by the obvious improvement.

Revision is the most effective teaching tool there is. It's one thing to preach detail in the abstract. It's another for a writer to discover, in her own story, that what made the stranger "scary" was "a white scar on the cheek and a jumping eye." Or that the sunset was "beautiful" because of the "streaks of gold blurring into pink, the red ball of the sun dropping behind the mountain."

Even those niggling corrections of spelling and punctuation are only contributing to clarity. They're eliminating distractions that get between the reader and the work.

Teachers and parents, you have revised, whether a letter or report, resume, even a shopping list. Show your students. Abraham Lincoln revised the Gettysburg Address. You can find it on the net.

Revision is where the real teaching takes place and takes hold. But it is a discipline, on your part as much as the students'. If your conviction flags—if you allow revision to slip from the positive back into the remedial—your students' will, too. Stigma is always lurking. For all my song and dance, I'm reconciled to my students proudly handing me their brilliant, transformational drafts—and saying, "I fixed it. Any more mistakes?"

Some tips:

Familiarize your students with your criteria even before their draft. Emphasize what matters to you about the activity, whether it's cause and effect, detail, beginnings or endings, imagery, alliteration, etc. Then revision reinforces your teaching.

Even a minute or two of one-on-one conferencing can bring dramatic results. But be selective in what you teach through the draft. Overwhelming the student with every possible improvement signals failure. Be patient. As a teacher, you have the entire school year to get to it all; as a parent, an entire childhood.

Build on what's positive in a draft. Aside from the morale boost, it's highly instructive to point out what's already working. If the hapless draft shows no virtues at all, invent what it *might* have been trying to accomplish.

Lead but don't compel. You may see possibilities in a draft that would expand the writer's grasp in exciting ways. Excellent, if the student is ready to follow you. If not, back off. Preserve the student's ownership of his writing.

Young students need a revision format. They aren't able to jot minute notes in the margins or between lines, especially if they're adding entire paragraphs. I introduce a symbol system. At each spot of insertion, the writer marks a different symbol, first a star, say, then a triangle, then a square, and so on. On another page, she writes out those revisions, in order, each identified with its matching symbol. (Whimsical variations may appear—a happy face, rainbow, the planet Saturn.) On final copy, the symbols remind the writer to add the new material.

Reality check: Occasionally the revisions make the story or poem worse, overdoing it, perhaps, or veering off on some woolly tangent. But the vast majority are real advances, and you have the whole year to hone the process.

Related note: Current standardized tests often require evidence of prewriting. Helpful as a nod to the writing process, tyrannical as a demand.

I find that prewriting serves students extremely well in expository forms. Webbing generates and supports ideas, and an outline orders the material. Graphic organizers such as charts or Venn diagrams are useful, too. I recommend those steps wholeheartedly.

On the other hand, while many young fiction writers and poets benefit from prewriting, others are ready to plunge straight into their drafts, and that impulsive momentum dies if they're forced to prewrite.

The fact that the student authors in *Here I Am a Writer* responded to classroom assignments, for the most part, might seem to diminish their achievements. It shouldn't. Their own creative energy overwhelms the initial prompt, obliterates it. And some wrote entirely independently, from their own impulses... because they were given the precious time to do so.

The marvel is, most didn't think of themselves as writers at all. They sat in rows of hard desks, or jostled elbows with their neighbors around tables, and—in the midst of their daily routines, under the murmur of an adjoining class still reciting Pledge, or the ticking of the omnipresent wall clock, or ruckus at the lunch bell—evoked wonder.

# Activities

*—Robert Arredondo*

# In My House

**EXAMPLES:** Adrianna Escalante, "*In Kari*—My House," p. 40; Marisa Yucupicio, "House of Water and Feathers," p. 55.

This is a sneaky introduction to surrealism, so grounded in the everyday that students won't notice it.

A home that one invents for one's self is a metaphor for one's state of being. Here I invite the students to become dream architects. For the sake of the class we define an architect as someone who designs buildings. I tell the class they're going to design their own homes, in writing. They're not ordinary architects, though, but dream architects. That is, instead of being built from the usual materials, such as brick, wood, sheetrock, concrete, etc., each part of the house will be made of whatever the student chooses. The walls could be clouds, for instance, the floor solid gold. The windows might be telescopes. The couch could be a live buffalo. Anything, as long as it's not the familiar, conventional material.

Together, we collect on the board possible elements of the house: roof, walls, windows, doors and knobs, floors, the various pieces of furniture, lights, porch. Other features may pop up: a doorbell, walkway, carport, yard, garden, etc.

In this case I tend not to use written models as a focus; the class discussion serves that purpose.

### Directions

*Describe your house, feature by feature. You don't need to include every possible item, but start by at least covering the basics of roof, walls, floor, and windows. Tell what each is made of. **Describe** it, how it looks at various times of day, for instance, what sounds it might make, what it feels like, or even smells or tastes like. What might that part of the house **do**, or how might it be **used**? **Why** is it made of whatever you chose?*

*Your writing could take the form of a story, how you*

*constructed your house, what happened with it. But it doesn't need to. The descriptions could be enough. Be spontaneous. Accept whatever comes into your head, as if it's a dream.*

*But this isn't just a list: the roof is bear fur, the floor is ice, the TV is a dragon's eye. Take your time to describe each part of the house. I'd rather see just five or six parts, well described, than a list of fifteen or twenty with no description.*

*No matter how hungry you are, don't make it all food. Let's have some variety.*

Given this opportunity, most students choose to write something positive, to them, at least; they're fantasizing an emotional environment that they desire. But be prepared for the occasional disturbing wreck of a house, with the paper roof caved in, demon-chairs that eat the inhabitants in gory detail, and so on. This could be a joke, or a sign of real distress on the part of the writer.

# Problem Story

**EXAMPLES:** Martín Acuña, "Holes," p. 43; Antone family, pp. 191-98.

Problems are the engine that drives most fiction. Think of classic works of literature or bestsellers, books for children, popular movies. Most derive their development, resolution, suspense from the working out of one or more problems. Problems equal conflict, that staple of the narrative arts. Problems/conflict can arise between characters, between a character and society, between characters and the forces of nature, within a character himself.

Nobody likes to have problems, I say, so why do people make stories and movies about them, and why do people read them and watch them?

Sensitive answers may emerge, such as "we feel bad" for the characters or "it reminds me of my own problems" or even "we're glad it's not us." All valid, but if it doesn't arise naturally, I also steer the class toward the most primal grip on an audience: we want to find out what happens. How does it turn out?

With younger students, I invite them to suggest possible problems they could write about, beginning with those in their own lives. Bike has a flat tire? Trouble with brother or sister?

Do older people have problems? Even teachers? Police? Star athletes or singers?

Animals?

Since this can be fiction, you could write about a shoe's problem, an alien's, a rock's.

Problem stories could be serious, profound. They could be ridiculous—someone woke up with a pickle for a nose.

I tell them the story could be true, or made up, or a combination of both.

We examine the different steps in following through a story about a problem, examining a model story or inventing one collectively. Though not written to this prompt, Marisa Yucupicio's

"The Frog Who Never Could Catch Flies" [p. 39] is, in fact, an excellent example of a problem story.

High school or middle school students need no help composing a litany of problems, so discussion here likely will focus on a model story, its skills, its impact, how it works itself out to a satisfying resolution. In Wenona Ortegas' "The Journey" [p. 145], the narrator's central problem is dealing with her father's death.

Whether the problem is solved or not is up to the writer. And real life reminds us that success or failure is not necessarily a matter of either-or.

A third grader, for instance, wrote a largely true story of his friend, whose skin condition led to his being mocked, which led to his getting into fights, having no friends, and being generally miserable. His mother had tried lotion and doctors, but the problem, and its ramifications, persisted. He made a friend who moved away.

Then the writer became his friend, and they have fun making up stuff together. The kid's skin still is bad, and people still call him names, but at least he has "more company."

A professional author could envy the nuance and wisdom of this ending. The problem isn't solved, but it's mitigated. It has become tolerable. Sometimes that's the most we can hope for.

### Directions

*What is the problem and who has it?* Older writers might offer a brief character sketch here, with accompanying detail describing the problem.

*Why is the problem important?* As with the hypothetical example of the coyote with a broken leg, I encourage writers to explore and describe the consequences, so we readers are convinced that the problem matters.

*What is done to try to solve the problem?* These may be efforts by the character herself, or by others. It could make the story more exciting if these initial attempts don't work (as with the boy and his skin condition). They could even make the problem worse.

*Finally, we want to know how it all turns out. Does the problem get solved? If so, how? If not, why not?* Not just—"the coyote's leg healed." We want the **how**. Did he languish in a cave, eating bugs and roots, until at last the leg was whole? Did he get himself adopted by a family who took care of him? Did he steal an ATV to run down his food until the bone mended? Did he check into the ER?

If the writer is relating a real-life problem, as yet unsolved, the ending might imagine how it might be solved.

As in real life, characters may fail to solve their problems. Or at least not solve them completely. We can be satisfied with a story even if the character isn't.

Like any story, this one is enriched by sensory detail, **especially during its most important parts**. Detail creates emphasis. A scene has more impact when we can see it, hear it, touch/feel it, even smell or taste it, in some cases. Use detail purposefully. We don't need five sensory details about a character's breakfast cereal, probably, but we might want at least that many about the climactic moment that solves, or fails to solve, the problem.

First drafts, especially by younger writers, often are sketchy on detail. Revision can help reinforce the uses of detail.

# Goal Story

**EXAMPLE:** Eucario Mendez, "Mr. John," pp. 70-71.

This is a variation on the problem story. Instead of a problem, we start with a character and a goal. We want to know why the goal is important to the character, what the character does to try to achieve the goal. We might want to know what obstacles could get in the way of the goal. Finally, we want to know if the character achieves the goal, and if so, how. If not, why not?

"Mr. John" is an excellent model for a class, in part for its humorous, expressive details.

# Legend

**EXAMPLE:** Marisa Yucupicio, "The Frog Who Never Could Catch Flies," p. 54.

This story has a clear form, which is pertinent if you're focusing your students on beginning, middle, end. At the same time it requires ingenuity and imagination in its problem-solving aspects. While I've taught it often to students as young as first grade, they may need help in getting over the initial bafflement of imagining things *not* as they are now.

Many cultures have an oral tradition of origin tales, how things got the way they are. If your students belong to such a culture, it's important to approach this activity with respect. Origin stories may bear a spiritual significance, and traditional stories often teach moral and social values, as well. To separate my role distinctly from those, I emphasize that we're doing the activity strictly for fun. At the opposite pole, I also stress that we're not looking for scientific explanations, but made-up stories. We're inventing legends.

Rudyard Kipling's *Just So Stories* are lighthearted explorations of the origin legend form.

I always begin this activity by telling or reading an origin story, careful not to repeat the disaster of my first ArtsReach residency with O'odham primary schoolers. If it's not the proper season for a traditional story or subject matter, I can always read Marisa's story of the frog. Not only is it sweetly engaging, but it also models form and the use of sensory detail.

After discussing the story's development, I suggest possible story subjects, inviting others from the class. I begin by focusing on animals with distinctive features, how the lion got his mane, how the turtle got its shell, how dogs came to bark, how the cheetah got its speed. Why cats land on their feet. Why pigs roll in mud. I include other phenomena, the sun, moon, and stars, effects of gravity, rainbows, geographical landmarks such as mountains or the Grand Canyon. I may even touch on more personal possibilities: how my cousin got his big feet. How my sister got smart.

### Directions

While discussing the model story, I write the three main parts on the board:

*Tell how things used to be.*

*Describe **how** things changed.*

*Tell how things were different afterward.*

Together, we explore how the model story fits that form. In "The Frog Who Never Could Catch Flies," the frog used to have a short tongue, which led to his being unable to hunt prey, which in turn left him hungry, bored, and friendless. We note the sensory description of the frog.

During the middle of the story, he gained his long tongue from the talking bush. Point out how the sensory descriptions of the bush, and the dialogue, enliven that scene. I linger on the **how** of the change. It's not "hey, presto, you've got a long tongue." The talking bush actually makes a tongue out of a stick—part of itself, we can guess. (Similarly, in the Pima legend of the rattlesnake's fangs, the sun makes those potent fangs from its powerful rays.)

The story ends with the frog enjoying his long tongue, which brings us back to the present, because frogs really do have long tongues. Now the frog can eat his fill. We know the frog is happy because Marisa, the writer *shows* us: he's singing.

Then students choose their own subjects.

For younger writers, I emphasize, *Frogs really have long tongues. In the beginning of the story, did the frog have a long tongue or a short tongue?*

*If you're writing a story about how the lion got his mane, in the beginning of your story did the lion have a mane? No. He had short hair, or maybe he was bald. What was it like for the lion, having no mane?*

*In a story of how humans got smart, were they smart at the*

234 Here I Am a Writer

*beginning? No, they were really dumb. Give examples of how dumb. What was it like for people, being so dumb?*

Young kids may need extra help getting over that disorienting hump: however things are now, at the beginning of the story things were not that way.

For the middle part of the story, I encourage different ways of effecting the change. For instance, in the case of a turtle getting its shell, it could fall backwards into an old pot, which becomes its shell (accidental). It could go to a crafts shop and construct one out of tiles, say (intentional). It could get help from a magical being or from other animals. *But whatever you choose, explain* **how**. *Go beyond: "It grew." "The wizard waved his wand."*

*For the ending, describe the life of your animal, or the state of the stars or rainbows or whatever, after the change took place. Show how things are different from before.*

In all parts of the "legend," detail greatly enhances the storytelling. Adding detail likely would be a focus of revision, as well, perhaps, as the **how** of the middle part.

# Grandparents as Kids

**EXAMPLES:** Josie Frye, "A Story About My Grandmother," p. 84; Regina Johnson-Eleando, "Grandmother," p. 191.

It may be hard for students to imagine that their grandparents once were the same age as themselves, equally challenging to grasp the world that their child-grandparents lived in, so long ago. But connecting with possible worlds, even those past, is what fiction does.

I begin with a math problem: in what year would your grandparent have been the same age you are now? For example, what if you are 11, your grandfather is an estimated 55, and the current year is 2009? Your grandfather would have been your present age 44 years ago, that is, in 1965.

That launches our discussion. Though ages will vary, most of the class will locate their child-grandparents within the same general decade, in this case the mid-60s. I can provide some mainstream touchstones of the period—the Cold War, Vietnam, civil rights movement. The astounding backwardness of technology (in these students' eyes)—no personal computers, ipods, cable TV, video-DVD, or video games. Instead, transistor radios. Drive-in movies. Schoolgirls in dresses. Often the classroom teacher will join in.

For a grandparent in a Mexican village, say, or a remote corner of a reservation, conditions will differ dramatically from my experience. Students may want to research at home, interviewing family members, before beginning to write the next day. Or the discussion may continue yet another day, postponing the writing further.

I tell the students they will be writing a fictional story about the grandparent. Some may be based in fact, with only the specific details imagined, others considerably altered from reality, others wholly imaginary. If a student is reluctant to invent fiction about an actual grandparent, the option is to create a fictional character of the same age, living at the same time, as that child-grandparent.

### Directions

I give these prompts at intervals, allowing time for writing in between. Students may not respond to all.

*Briefly describe the weather on the day your story takes place.*

*Describe the specific setting. Not just "Mexico," for example, but "a cornfield in a valley surrounded by mountains" or "sitting around the dinner table."*

*Describe what the grandparent is doing. What is he wearing?*

*Something unexpected happens. What is it?*

The "unexpected" might involve a new character, such as a visitor, an incident with an animal, a phenomenon of weather, an accident or discovery by the main character, or some more rogue element. It could come from outside or within the opening situation. "Unexpected" is deliberately broad. One student decided rabbits would start raining from the sky.

*In a story, as in real life, everything that happens makes other things happen. That is cause and effect. There can be chain reactions of effects, where A causes B, and B causes C, and so on. That's how many stories develop. Whatever unexpected event happened in your story will cause other things to happen. Follow your story and see where it leads, and ends. Take the time to concentrate on sensory details.*

More open-ended than other story formats in this portfolio, this activity can require more individual coaching, but the rewards are worth it.

# The Girl Who Turned into a Horse

**EXAMPLE:** Patrick Lewis-Jose, "The Boy and the Eagle," pp. 162-63.

This activity has become my paradigm for adapting stories into lessons. Touching upon a universal fascination, transformation, it has proven accessible and appealing to all ages. It breaks down into easily recognizable stages. Writers can fill the form with whatever emotional content they need, bend or break the form, or as in any of my creative writing activities, abandon it altogether.

We start with my retelling of a simple story, passed on to me by an ArtsReach colleague, Pam Uschuk. It's based on a traditional Plains Indian tale.

An old storytelling lady tells one about a girl who turned into a horse. The lady says a girl went down to the river to get water in a bucket, because her parents told her to. But while she was there a man asked her to go eat dinner with him. The girl left the bucket behind and went off with him.

The man turned himself and her into horses and ran away with her. Her parents searched everywhere, but they couldn't find her.

After two years, they finally found her, and when they did, she turned back into a girl again. But her hair was long and tangled up, and her feet were as hard as rocks.

I ask the students why they think the girl's hair was long and tangled up, and why her feet were as hard as rocks. There are no right or wrong answers, I tell them. We're just guessing.

Many students will theorize that she's still part horse. The long, tangled hair is like the mane, while the hard feet indicate hooves or horseshoes. She didn't completely turn back.

Others look to her experiences. Nobody brushed her hair

for two years, while wind and branches messed it up. Her feet got hard from running on stones, hot sand, sticks, and cactus.

Still others blend the two approaches.

If no one else does, I may add a third, metaphorical level of meaning. Here's a girl who skipped her chore and left everything to run off with a guy. That sounds pretty wild, and the long, tangled hair suggests emotional wildness. To live wild, away from her family, for two years also requires toughness, like those hard feet.

To me, the fundamental truth of the story is that experiences change us. I give an example from my own life. As a child, I always had girlfriends. In nursery school, ignorant of the ways of love, I threw a tin cup at Holly's head to get her attention. In kindergarten, I rode the bus with Deirdre. In second...and so on. Until my parents got divorced, when I was in seventh grade. Bang. No more girlfriends for four years. "It wasn't conscious," I tell my classes. "But something in me decided, 'I don't want any part of this.'" I encourage students to recall major events in their lives, moving to a different school, a parent losing a job, or getting a great new job, and what changes resulted in people's circumstances, behavior, feelings.

If conflict is the engine of fiction, change is the destination. For fiction writers, "The Girl Who Turned into a Horse" in an archetype.

So, for the horse-girl, her change was physical. To expand the story's implications, I ask what other ways she might have changed. Does she eat differently, act differently, speak differently? How about her dreams, or her feelings about horses?

### Directions

*Tell how the person was turned into something else. What was it?* For older students, I also ask for background on the character and setting. I throw out various ways the person could be changed: a potion, a spell, drinking or bathing in poisoned water, being pricked or bitten by something, being hit by lightning, dreaming or yearning one's way into something else. Details will intensify this dramatic moment.

The character could be the writer herself, a famous person, a fictional character, an acquaintance. If the writer chooses a friend from the class, I require, as with practically all stories, that she invent a fictional name. Your friend might not want to become a sea slug, I point out. More generally, the use of friends' names distracts from the story itself and quickly can ignite a fad.

*Describe what it was like being that new thing.* This phase is barely covered in my brief "Horse" model, so I dwell on it. If the person is now a meteor, for instance, describe its color, the sensation of hurtling through space. What do you see around you? If a shark, how does the light look under water? How does the water feel? For an ant, how does the world look from way down there? What sounds does it hear?

Writers decide if their person has completely lost himself in this new being, or still retains his human mind, memories, and so on. Patrick Lewis-Jose decided his eagle was an apprentice, needing practice in eagle ways.

Does the python, for example, still live in its own home and attempt to go to school, or does it slither off in search of the jungle?

What does this being do? What happens in its new life?

How does the vanished person's family feel?

*After the person turned back, how was he/she different from before?* Recall our discussion around the ending of the horse-girl's story. How has it affected your character, having been a meteor, shark, ant, python, or whatever? Physically, or emotionally, or in his habits, mannerisms, beliefs? In "The Boy and the Eagle," we get the wonderful lingering feathers, the astounding two hearts. Not only has the character been much affected, but in his absence, his family has changed, too; he has a new baby brother.

Some writers don't want their characters to resume human form. In that case, I ask they end their stories by explaining or showing why that is.

I base many writing activities on stories. The Labors of Hercules. Folk tales from around the world. Hamlet. Modern fiction. Newspaper articles, or bizarre tabloid concoctions. My own personal stories. Some I practice telling, some I read. Often I use student examples, such as Marisa Yucupicio's "The Frog Who Never Could Catch Flies."

I look for universal themes that resonate. Hercules' *goal* was to free himself from slavery. The *labors* were his means, his challenge, the story. His *reward* was the life of a hero, eventually immortality as a constellation in the sky. Hamlet embodies *indecision*. From an African tale of a woman who was made of oil, we can extrapolate stories about *people made of weird stuff*—glue, fire, steel, pretzel sticks, gravity, and so on.

In high school, I met a girl at a student night club. I accompanied her and her group to a friend's house, miles south of my own. Busting my curfew by four hours, I arrived home to a silent street, dark save for one light—my mother's bedroom. She cried hysterically, having thought I was dead, and spanked me for the last time in my life, with a hairbrush. The theme I extract from this is *transgression*, breaking your society's rules. A society can be your country, state, city, tribe, church, team, group of friends, household. *What leads to the transgression? Tell the story of how it occurs. What are the consequences, both to the transgressor and the society whose rules were broken?* In my case, for instance, after the initial punishment I was grounded for two weeks. I lost my mother's trust. And I gained a girlfriend (my first in the four years since my parents' divorce, as it happens). Outcomes are not always morally neat. For that matter, look at Martin Luther King, Jr., Cesar Chavez, Nelson Mandela—transgressors all.

# People in My Life (poem)

**EXAMPLES:** Sonja Blackowl, "An Indian Girl," p. 129; Yolanda Darrell, "Leilani," p. 138.

## Teaching Poetry

Poetry is not like stories or other prose, such as reports. Poetry even looks different on the page. Rather than blocks of paragraphs, poems unfold line by line, with deliberate breaks, sometimes after only a few words.

While famous narrative poems tell stories—the *Iliad* and *Odyssey, Paradise Lost*—the poems I present generally do not. They are meditations, perceptions, emotions, riffs, existing in a timeless now. Ande Escalante's story "The Cowboy" (p. 31) moves through time toward a resolution. In contrast, her poem "Yaqui Words" (p. 28), has no before or after. It moves through associations in Ande's mind.

Poems, I often tell students, are like really smart dreams. Anything can happen. The mind flows where it wants, from association to association, according to an underlying emotional or cognitive need. The words capture the reader in the dream.

Most students know Kool-Aid. A story is like the Kool-Aid powder dissolved in water, drunk in a glass one sip or gulp after another, filling and satisfying. A poem is like the Kool-Aid powder licked plain, concentrated, intense.

Poetry is sound. Rhyme is the best-known instrument of poetic music, though many great poems don't rhyme. Rhythm can please equally, as in the cadences of Josie Frye's "Is it 'I Am' or 'My Name'" (p. 88). Syntax is music, too. See Marvin Lewis, Jr.'s "Because" (p. 114). Opening with doggerel, the poem soars into phrasing of pure longing. It is like a leap from childhood to adulthood within a single sentence.

Often I suggest that students fold their paper in half to write their poems. They're welcome to stray over that midline, but it reminds them they're not creating stories, with their blocks of paragraphs, but poems, one image, thought, phrase, or even word at a time.

For this poem, I focus on a significant person in the poet's life, then on an action that helps reveal that person's character. This poem depends on attention to specific detail as a way of capturing an essence of the person.

For instance, the impact of Yolanda's poem, "Leilani," lies in the details that compress meaning into images. To the child, her bare feet denote freedom, to the anxious observer, vulnerability. Leilani's hair swings free—but Yolanda imagines it snagging painfully on a branch.

Simile expands the power of image, as when the child is likened to a sponge "soaking up life." But in Sonja's poem about Yolanda herself, that human subject almost disappears into a whirlwind of similes, as the poem ascends into a spiritual dimension. We are caught up in the solemn ecstasy of the dance, Yolanda's "prayer."

Each poem has found its own way into meaning, through close detail and the imaginative use of language.

### Directions

We read and discuss a model poem or two, calling attention to sensory detail, simile, and pleasures of form and sound.

I invite the class to think of people who are important to them, probably in positive ways, though not necessarily. Friends, family members, or other figures in their lives.

*This poem is about an important person in your life, doing something that matters to him or her.* What people do, and how, expresses much about what they are like. These activities could be vigorous, such as skateboarding, or quiet, such as reading or even napping. Usually students will choose what their subject likes, such as eating pizza, but it could be what he hates, such as vacuuming.

*The poem will focus simply on the person doing that particular activity, in detail. What does your mother's hair do as she leans over the stove, stirring the pot? What sound does the rim make as your brother slams the basketball through? What happens to your friend's body as he plays his video game? What does his face look like? What original similes could you use to help describe it?*

*Remember, this isn't a story. We don't care how it turns out. Just concentrate on the action itself, and the person doing it.*

I encourage students to fold their paper in half, lengthwise, and in younger classrooms, demonstrate how to do it. *Think one line at a time. Don't worry if you don't know the entire poem when you begin. That's good. Trust yourself to discover where the poem will go, one line at a time. Remember: detail. That's what makes the poem.*

## Revision

Because poems are concentrated and delicate, revision requires a light touch. Stories may benefit from adding huge chunks of material, but the shape and sound of a poem will tear if altered too much. Revise on the level of word, phrase, image, simile. *Find the truest, most expressive word. If you have a horse "go" down a hill, can you think of a better verb?* Students will substitute "gallop," "prance," or even "slide" or "tumble." Each would be an improvement.

*Look for the descriptive words that sharpen your effect. Because a poem is so finely tuned, even one descriptive word can transform it.* A second grader invoked "the dark angel that watches over us." *How does it feel if I say "an angel watches over us"?* Most students respond, "good," "safe," something along that line. *What if "a **dark** angel watches over us"?* "Creepy." "Scary." "Evil."

Often I will ask for a description where there is none, or for the student to attempt a simile. The writers can try out phrases on a scratch sheet, then select the favorite version.

Initially, I only dared teach poetry at all thanks to Mick

Fedullo's curriculum, *It's Like My Heart Pounding.* I'm a fiction writer, not a poet. It probably shows. But that didn't stop my students from writing sensational poems. There, you see? Even an amateur can do this.

# Time of Day Poem

**EXAMPLES:** Josie Frye, "Rain," p. 87; Marvin Lewis, Jr., "The Day Is Bright Light," p. 113 and "Night, Morning," p. 115 ; Yolanda Darrell, "Sunrise," p. 125; Regina Johnson-Eleando, "Baboquivari," p. 189.

Nothing is more commonplace than our daily passage through day and night. Yet it requires only a moment's pause to appreciate the vastness of cosmological forces at work. From the swing of heavenly bodies through space to the shadow of a flywing on a leaf, our cycle of light and dark has held mystical sway over viewers since humans first left their mark.

A poem can be that momentary pause. The model poems trap flickers of that awe. They do so humbly, fixing on the ordinary details until they give up their hidden dimensions. Details, again, and daring associations, deeply personal similes.

## Directions

In discussion I touch on these mysteries, illustrating with one or two model poems. The poets trusted their imaginations, I say. They let details, similes, and language lead the way, taking whatever came.

*We're going to write poems about a particular place, at a particular time of day, during a particular season of the year. Think of the differences in that place between day, night, sunrise, nigh noon, dusk; and between winter, spring, summer, fall.* (Josie Frye's "Rain," for instance, could take place only during a summer monsoon.) *Those are the first decisions to make. What place? When, during the year? What time of day?*

*How does the time of day affect that specific place? The lighting, coloring, temperature, what is happening to the sky, landscape, maybe plants and animals. Close your eyes and picture it in your mind. Listen, too, feel, maybe smell, even taste.*

*Write those details. Let your imagination run free. Allow*

*anything that comes to mind into your poem. Don't worry if it*
*makes sense. Lead with your senses, and follow wherever they go.*

Creative writing of all kinds elevates our involvement with
life. Most of the stories and poems in this book would not exist
had not a teacher asked for them. Ask your students and children
to do that for themselves. Ask. Those stories and poems have been
given to you. You opened yourself to them. Now pass them on.

⊙  ⊙  ⊙  ⊙  ⊙  ⊙

# Afterword

As a record of its subjects' lives, *Here I Am a Writer* was obsolete even before I began writing it. Life doesn't stand still, obviously. I'm aware of significant changes, unaware of countless others, I'm sure. Already I've lost touch with some of those who could update or correct me. I never could catch up even if I tried. These are only stories, impressions left by past events. Then again, as stories they are reborn every time someone reads them.

Please visit Christopher McIlroy online at:
www.mcilroywritingservices.com

## About Christopher "Kit" McIlroy

Christopher McIlroy teaches writing through schools and communities, and local colleges in the Tucson, Arizona area. In 1987 he helped found ArtsReach, a writing program targeted toward Native American communities in southern Arizona, and occasionally in other areas. He also developed an author-in-residence program through the Tucson Unified School District. McIlroy has taught fiction and composition through the University of Arizona and the MFA Program for Writers at Warren Wilson College and Pima Community College. He holds an MFA in fiction writing from the University of Arizona and received a National Endowment for the Arts Fellowship, two Arizona Writers Fellowships, and an Arizona Commission on the Arts Artist Project Grant. His story collection *All My Relations* won the Flannery O'Connor Award for Fiction, and the title story was included in *Best American Short Stories*.

CPSIA information can be obtained at www.ICGtesting.com
Printed in the USA
BVOW031914231212

308959BV00001B/10/P